AT HOME IN THE UNIVERSE

From the Siberian Steppes to Baltimore

An Autobiography
by
Oscar E. Bonny

ICARUS BOOKS: BALTIMORE

To Marjorie and Monroe Freeman with kindest regards — O. E. Bonny

AN ICARUS AUTOBIOGRAPHY

Published by ICARUS BOOKS
1015 Kenilworth Drive, Baltimore, MD 21204

Cover Design by James Toarello

Library of Congress Catalogue Number: 89-080519
ISBN: 0-944806-01-5

PREFACE

This is the story of my life. A story of a brief and sunny childhood. It is a story of catastrophe, fear, persecution, escape and death. It is the story of a struggle for freedom from tyranny, from ignorance, from poverty and from cultural and political bondage. It is a story of hunger, nakedness and hope. It is a story of loneliness and of love and romance. It is a story of inferiority and its conquest. It is the story of war between two worlds as they met in conflict on military battle fields and in the soul and mind of a child. It is a story of the religious distortions of fundamentalism and a Biblical literalism.

Beyond this, it is a story of millions of uprooted people, caught between the millstones of titanic forces, driven from place to place, homeless and destitute. It is the story of people without a country, and without roots in the social structure which gives meaning and purpose to existence. For many of these victims the struggle became too hard, the road too long. A benevolent darkness settled over their lives, shielding them forever from the further ravages of time. It is a story written in partial reply to the last request of my oldest brother, Erich, who had hoped to write the story of our family, but whose plans were interrupted by a premature death.

In retracing the movements of my family, from the comforts of my present home, it seems incredible that we should have survived, and that all of this should have happened in one brief lifetime.

— Oscar E. Bonny

Gratitude is due to my wife, Jane, and my daughter Beatrice Starrett, who have read and improved the manuscript; to my niece, Peggy Bonney Griffith, who made further corrections and typed the mnanuscript; to David Diorio who saw the matter through to its final publication, and to his dear wife, Margaret, who provided tea and conversation during our discussions.

MY CREED

That man is a success who has lived well, laughed often, and loved much; who has gained the respect of intelligent men and the love of little children; who has filled his niche with dignity and accomplished his task; who has never lost his sense of wonder at the incredible mystery of Nature and Life; who is able to leave his spot on earth in a better condition than he found it, whether through an inspiring word, a loving deed or a gentle touch; who looked for the best in others and gave the best he had.

TABLE OF CONTENTS

ILLUSTRATIONS

To
ERICH
My oldest brother
Whose last request it was that this
story be written

Chapter 1

THE ROAD INTO EXILE

The magic word America came to me for the first time when I, a child of five and my brother Erich, who was two years older, were playing in a parish garden in Poland in June of 1915. My father was minister of a German Baptist church in a small German-speaking village south-east of Warsaw. Mr. Fenske, a dear friend of the family, had just returned from America where he had become familiar with an instrument designed for the enjoyment of the leisure moments of life, and one entirely new to us. It was a swing designed to accomodate a number of people seated facing each other on two seats; by pushing with the feet at a ribbed flooring, the swing would move gently to and fro. Mr. Fenske had asked father's permission to build one in the parish garden, to be enjoyed by the family as well as by the parishioners. Erich and I kept a close vigil, waiting for the time it would be finished and we would be able to initiate it. We swung so heartily on our first trial that Erich, who was a bit plump, had the misfortune of falling underneath it, while I kept on swinging in the hope that he would eventually emerge. He did, but by that time even our mother hardly recognized him.

That was our first introduction to America. All it meant was an overgrown but fascinating toy in our garden. But this new bit of pleasure was soon to end. War, which had broken out a year before, was soon to end the few happy years of my childhood and plunge the entire family, and countless other people, into a nightmare of exile, persecution, homelessness, and desperate hunger. My own conscious memories of Krobanosch are of the flowers in our garden, the sundial, the swing, and the childhood games. For the rest, I rely upon my father's family history, written in the 1950's. But I am sure that the pain, suffering, and sense of dislocation, observed or experienced, left a permanent mark upon my personality.

By 1915 the entire male population of our village between the ages of 21-45, their wagons and horses, had been mobilized. Thus, except for my father who was exempt as a clergyman, only women, children and older men remained. Since the then Austrian border was not far to the south of us and the Germans had made significant advances, there were times when we could hear the cannons on the front, and the sky at night was turned into a red glow by the light of burning villages. Wounded began to arrive from the front, and our village became a hospital center. My father writes of mangled bodies, often with missing limbs, of soldiers praying for help and others asking to be put out of their misery. Our parsonage bacame the headquarters for two officers and a doctor. One night a youth just drafted came to father to ask him to kneel with him in prayer in the pew where he had always worshipped in since he was uncertain he would ever return. Traffic on the highway passing the village was endless day and night, crowded with soldiers, war materiel, and people fleeing from their homes.

The superstition of the largely illiterate Russian and Polish soldiers was boundless. One day a piece of wire was discovered in one of the wells in the village. This immediately led to the conclusion that the German owner of the property must be using it to communicate with the approaching Germans. The man was brutally beaten in the hope of extracting information about his secret. Father's choir director, it was discovered, was in possession of a tuning fork. I do not know what the unfortunate consequences were for the choir director, but father, who was also in possession of a similar, subversive instrument, buried it the next night in a place known only to himself.

Russia, ill-prepared for war, was unable to hold the line. Straggling remnants of ill-equipped soldiers were in retreat. Each day the front moved closer, and the noise of war spread terror in traditionally peaceful communities. It was also rumoured that some of the freight trains contained human cargo on their way east.

While the older people were agonizing over the future, the children continued their play. Erich and I had decided that it would be good for June bugs to have a home of their own, so that they would have a place to sleep at night. So we collected boards and built a small lean-to on the sunny side of the church, and spent hours collecting a variety of creatures and placing them in their new home. It had been a beautiful Saturday afternoon, bathed in sunshine. Before the work could be completed, mother called us in for dinner. Without knowing it then, that was to end the brief sunny years of my early life, a time and place to which we would never be able to return. We were to be engulfed in the irrational passions sweeping over all of Europe, shattering the dreams of childhood and the hopes of our parents.

The next day, Sunday, was just as beautiful. Father, as always, was in the pulpit in his swallow-tail suit and a shirt with celluloid collar and cuffs. The outfit was a gift from a friend who felt that a minister should look more distinguished than others. The church was filled to capacity; there was too much uncertainty, people were seeking a security earth could not provide. The choir had sung the anthem and father had just begun his sermon. Suddenly a messenger from the nearest government office burst into the sanctuary, keeping silent until father had completed his sermon before making his announcement. According to a decree issued in the name of Tsar Nicholas, the village was to be evacuated to the interior of Russia! The closing hymn was never sung. Father ended the service with a prayer. The people wept and embraced each other to gain courage. They were to leave behind their homes and most of their belongings, meager though they were, and step out into the unknown. Slowly they left the sanctuary, only to linger in the beautiful floral garden mother had cultivated around the church. They were reluctant to separate; they needed each other in this time of crisis.

Father had slipped through the door in the chancel which opened into his study. When mother and we children arrived, we found him still on his knees. When he arose, we embraced and wept. What was to become of us? Then they took the two younger children, Erwin, three, and Alma, then one year old, into their arms and tried to explain to Erich and me what the messenger had said in the church.

What followed in the village during the next two days was a chaotic nightmare for all. We children wanted to take along the American swing and how could we leave behind the beautiful life-like spotted rocking-horse given us by a friend, and, incidentally, the only factory-made toy we were ever to have as children? There was the beautiful flower garden with its labyrinthine walks between circles and heart-shaped flower beds, which we had helped mother to build. There was father's home-made sundial by which all could tell the time of day. And what of our treasured fruit trees? Father had so valued his orchard that he had taken special measures to protect it from marauding Polish neighbours, who had no fruit trees. He would stretch a string along the fence when the fruit was ripe, and the string ended in his bedroom. Anyone scaling the fence came in touch with the string, which would pull the frying pan attached to it on the floor at father's bedside. In minutes father would confront the culprit. As a result, many rumours circulated through the Polish community about father's connection with Satan! Then there was our tiny black and white dog, who often got his Sunday pleasure by chasing the cat into the attic of the church during morning worship; mother would need to leave the choir to interrupt the mischief-makers. What was to become of them?

But the parents and the community at large had to face grimmer matters. They had to plan for survival, to think of food, clothing, bedding, utensils and other necessities. To gain a little cash, people started selling some furniture and livestock, but the Poles soon realized that if they refused to buy, in two days they could have what they wanted without paying for it. They even insisted on returning some of their purchases and recovering their money. Each family had to decide what dear possessions would have to be left behind; what they could, they hid in walls and under floors or buried in the ground. Other things were packed and then had to be abandoned at the roadside, when there was not enough room on the wagons which the local Polish peasants had to provide for our transportation.

The Tsar's decree was executed as promptly as it had been given. Soldiers moved into the village and rounded up all the German-speaking inhabitants, and herded them into the center of the village. Any straggler who could not decide what was to be left behind was prodded along. Early in the morning of July 9, 1915 the wagons had been loaded and the caravan was set in motion.

Our family at that time consisted of mother, father, us four children, and also our mother's father, Grandpa Zozmann. It was his misfortune to have been visiting us on the Sunday the decree was issued. Although he lived only fifteen miles away, he was not allowed to return to his family and was thus doomed to exile with us. Before we separated from the world we loved, father had us kneel around the table, which was daily practice both morning and evening. After the prayer, we embraced, wept, and said farewell to our home. For some time we could still see our church and the parsonage; then only the village; then distance separated us forever from the life we knew. We were set adrift, not knowing where we were going.

Those for whom there was no room on the wagons walked to Chelm, the closest railroad station. When we got there, we found the station so congested with uprooted humanity that it was impossible to get to the platform, let alone secure passage. The soldiers sent us to the next railroad center in Korbin, one hundred miles away. The procession moved slowly; many had to walk, horses had to be fed, and cows, which some farmers had taken along, had to be pastured and milked. Thus initially was milk provided for the small children, including those of our family. Mother had dried sacks of bread to keep it from spoiling. Meat had been boiled, packed into pails and covered with fat to protect against spoilage. We also had a primus, a little three-legged kerosene stove, which we managed to keep with us all the way to Siberia and which rendered inestimable service both then and later. In some villages the government had set up soup kitchens, where refugees were served borscht from large kettles. At night stakes were driven into the ground, and blankets stretched over them to provide some shelter against wind and rain.

When we arrived in Korbin the same conditions prevailed, so we were taken to the forest of Voldava. Even here others had already arrived before us; we became just another camp among many. Here we were to remain for weeks. Children were born and died, and here some of the oldest members of this wretched band of humanity, for whom the ordeal had been too difficult, found their graves. Since the camp was guarded and no one was allowed to leave, the dead had to be buried in the forest. Some, troubled by their inability to bury loved ones in sanctified grounds, moved them in the night and left them on the doorstep of a resident family, in the hope that they would be buried in a cemetery.

It is important to know that the reason for our evacuation of Krobanosch was never given. But we could assume that our "crime" was that we were of German origin and used the German language, and thus we represented a danger in the face of the advancing German army. It is ironic that in many instances the father or sons of the family were already serving in the Russian Army, while their wives and children were being sent into exile. In some areas, we heard that the men had been evacuated first and the women and children sent later to a different destination; many never found each other again.

While living in the forest, we could hear the guns of approaching armies. Rumour had it that the forces of Hindenburg were marching across Austria. Hope ran high at the camp that we might be overtaken by the Germans and not have to go into Russian exile. By bribing the guards the camp elders thought to prolong our stay in the forest in the hope of a rescue, but that day never came.

As food ran out, the cows had to be butchered, thus depriving the children of their milk supply. Life became grimmer by the day. It was at this time that I wandered off into the forest away from the camp. A frantic search began. It was not until nightfall that some one came upon me, got my name and returned me to camp. When I was asked where I was going, I replied that I was hungry and wanted to go home. How true this childhood quest for home was to become of my life. In some sense I never found my home again. Wherever the circumstances of life have placed me, I have ever been haunted by the feeling that this really is not my home, that I belong somewhere else.

Father never lost an opportunity to keep hope alive. When weather permitted, he held daily worship service in the forest. The time for worship was signaled when a group of men would climb to the top of a hill in the forest and start singing. People, terrified by the forces that threatened their survival, would flock to the service from nearby camps. Some of them acknowledged that they had never felt a need for the church, but that they were now discovering its meaning for their life. Father was an effective preacher, but what perhaps touched them even more deeply was the singing. This great chorus under the green canopy of trees touched life at its deepest level and inspired courage and hope.

When orders came to move, nearby peasants were again pressed into service to transport us to the railroad station at Korbin. When we arrived we again found a mass of people, civilians, soldiers, and war casualties. When freight cars were available, our villagers were loaded, some thirty people to a car. Before the sliding doors were closed and the train started to move, as many people as could stood in the door to take one last look at their part of the world. They spontaneously broke out into the anthem, *Es erglanzt uns von ferne ein Land.* (There is a home that is fairer than gold). Some people in the crowd outside joined in and many wept. Then the doors were closed.

The cars stunk of horse manure. What had been designed for cattle and freight was now to incarcerate humans. Planks had been arranged around the walls for sitting and sleeping. There were no sanitary facilities. The only light penetrating the darkness came through four holes near the top of the cars, but these were closed most of the time to prevent escape. Families placed their meager possessions into little piles and sat upon them. For a time life seemed paralyzed. No one knew quite what to do. There was little conversation, children began to cry, some people prayed, others wept and some sat in sullen resignation. Night was falling as the freight cars began to beat out their monotonous rhythm on tracks that crossed the Eurasian continent. No one had been told their destination. But since the train moved eastward, there were ominous words whispered: Siberia, exile to Siberia.

When the train stopped at some of the stations, the doors were opened and people were permitted to leave the cars to take care of their physical needs. At some stations this meant going into the woods; at others large square ditches had been dug and surrounded by a fence, and people had to crouch on slimy planks. The stench was indescribable. Sometimes the train would start before everyone had been able to return to his car, and one could watch men, women and children running with pants in hand trying to get onto the moving train. It must have been under these circumstances that I developed a life-long obsession never to be late for an appointment. Meals consisted largely of dried bread and hot water supplied at some of the stations. Sometimes there was a little meat. As long as there was any money left, it was possible to buy fruit and black bread from peasant women along the tracks.

The engine was fired with cords of wood of which there was not always a sufficient supply; then passengers were made to collect the additional fuel. Sometimes the train could not quite make an elevation in the tracks and soldiers or refugees had to provide extra energy by pushing. Chugging along about ten to twelve miles an hour or left standing on a siding for hours to allow a military train to pass, time became endless. Days were gray, since there was only the light that came through cracks, and nights were black. It was difficult to remember what day it was.

After we had passed a few stations and the train stopped, there was a representative of a well-to-do former member of the Krobanosch church waiting for my father. He was to take our family off the train so that my father could become the minister of a German-speaking community established near the Ukraine border. It had taken considerable effort and searching to locate the correct train. Anxious moments followed. There was much discussion and prayer. If father accepted the invitation, our family would be spared Siberian exile. But was it right "for a shepherd to forsake his sheep"? His people begged him not to leave them. It was a terribly difficult decision, but mother and father decided to follow their people into exile. The well-meant emissary had to leave disappointed. But the man he represented did not forget us; a number of times he sent father money in Siberia, wanting to assure himself that father would continue in his ministry and "not have to do menial work for a living".

The train journey became more hazardous. Because of lack of sanitary facilities, the terrible heat in the box car, lack of ventilation, and inadequate nourishment, illness began to spread. The most dreaded was cholera, called "black death" because infected persons turned black and were thus foretold of their death. My vivid recollection from this nightmare was of the men with black rubber gloves, who would open the doors at major stations to remove those who had died. Sometimes those only near death would be thrown into the same carts, since they were not expected to live much longer. They all shared a common grave.

One of the great difficulties which arose under these circumstances was to try to hide the critically ill before the doors were opened. The horror of this became especially real for us when mother came down with cholera, and for days her life hung in the balance. To hide her suffering body from the eyes of the "death men" friends in the car would throw blankets over her and "sit" on her as on a bench, when we approached a station. With the help of father's knowledge of homeopathic medicine, the crisis passed and mother recovered. Another family in the car took a different way out. The father of a sick little boy decided he would go no farther. When the train stopped some distance from the station, with the help of friends, he threw out the body of his brother-in-law, who had already died, and all his meager possessions, and then got out with the sick child and his other son. The train moved on, leaving them behind. Much later my father learned that father and sons survived. As a very sensitive child I experienced all of this suffering with the keenest sensibility; observed quietly every detail of human pain and grief; and wondered why people should have to suffer so much.

One day when the train stopped and we were allowed to emerge into the open, we were confronted by giant mountains. I had never seen anything that tall. Their majesty was simply overpowering. The base was covered with a black pine forest while the top was covered in glistening snow. We were in the Ural Mountains. We were now at the border of Asia, at Orenberg. We had heard previously that from there we would go to Tashkent, near the Persian border where it was very hot. However, now we learned that Tashkent was closed to refugees because of a cholera epidemic. Instead we were to cross the Urals into Siberia. The trip through the Urals was for us children a very exciting trip. With the ventilators open we were aware that we were entering a dark tunnel. When we emerged into the light, grown-ups would hold us up to peer out of the ventilators and we would see a beautiful green valley. Then back into a dark tunnel we would go, to be followed by another green valley, and so on for about six hundred miles into Asia.

Route travelled by Oscar Bonny and his family. Loaded in cattle cars, the family left (1) Krobanosch, Poland in June, 1915, arriving in (2) Fjedorofka, Siberia, in July, 1915. They fled to (3) Horstchick, Ukraine in October, 1920, then to (4) Moscow in August, 1926, to (5) Riga, Latvia in September, 1926, then to London in October, 1926, and Saskatchewan, Canada in May, 1927.

Chapter 2

SIBERIA

Far beyond the Urals, after a trip of some three thousand miles, we arrived at the village of Fjedorofka on the Siberian steppes. After the train had stopped, we remained locked in our box cars for hours before the doors were finally opened and an officer told us to unload. What a relief to emerge into the fresh air of Siberia, to leave the suffocating odor of the cars, and to fill our lungs with clean air. A soldier informed us that we had reached our destination and that wagons would soon arrive from the nearby village to take us to our new "home."

So this was Siberia, the horizonless territory, one-tenth of the earth's total land mass, the land that had swallowed up nameless millions ever since Peter the Great in 1710 sent the first contingent of undesirables in their chains to Siberia. Successive tsars followed his example, and when the age of dictators came, the lines grew longer and longer. Under Stalin, Siberia became the bottomless cemetery.

For him, Siberia was the equivalent of Hitler's gas chambers, long before Hitler invented his. The millions who marched to their deaths here will never be known, nor how they died, for their suffering often defied the descriptive capacity of human language. Dostoyevsky, who had spent years here, called his gulag "The House of the Dead." Some of these were criminals, but many of them were intellectuals, people of independent thought, artists, and conscientious objectors to an inhuman political system.

But this was 1915 and the time of the last Tsar. We had arrived at this fearsome place. What was to become of us? Father had his faith, and he assured us that God would protect us. I shall not dwell on the entire scope of our five years in Siberia. My father has told the story in considerable detail. Rather, I shall touch upon details of my personal experience and those aspects which were important at the time, when I was between the ages of five and ten, or seem of interest and significance in retrospect.

We arrived in a village of one thousand inhabitants, already greatly over-crowded, but the soldiers demanded that additional room be found for us. Some in our group were convinced that we were being turned over to a "bunch of criminals." But we were soon to learn that this was far from the case. Here were people of compassion, unselfishness, and helpfulness, characteristics so common among a people who were forced to share a common fate and who had to depend on each other. Over the years we were to see ample evidence of this; without it we would not have survived.

One of these "criminals" offered father a small two-room hut in his backyard. It had once been used as a bakery, and was now to provide an immediate shelter for our family. It was entirely built of clay—walls, floor and roof. Each room had one small window just above the ground. There was a large clay oven in the front room. These ovens are a unique Siberian institution. They are used for cooking and baking during the day, and as a bed for the children at night. Here all of us children slept, especially in winter, when its warmth supplemented our body heat. The only fuel in these endless barren steppes was grass or straw in the summer and bricks in the winter. The bricks were made by mixing manure with straw, pounding it into a large flat sheet, then cutting it into bricks and storing it for the cold weather. Incidentally, one of the drawbacks of our living arrangement was the lice which also had a tendency to gravitate to the only warm spot in the house, and had to be accommodated in the same crowded area of the kitchen.

I soon discovered another hazard of this stove-centered existence. Much of my sleeping hours as a child were filled with gruesome nightmares which consisted of bombings, explosions, fire, ghosts, and corpses. Sometimes the situation would become so unbearable that I would start screaming and leave the bed in my sleep in search of a more congenial world. One night as I started out on my quest, I stepped from the stove into space and landed with one foot in a tea kettle of hot water. This brought me to my senses and my screams brought my parents to the rescue.

They had difficulty extricating my foot from the kettle. This experience added one more subject to my nocturnal agenda: the possibility of drowning in a tea kettle filled with hot water. Nightmares continued to haunt me, no doubt reflecting the cruelty I had observed around me. It was not until I was about thirty that these subsided.

With six long months of winter, the nights seemed endless and the cold sometimes unbearable. The stove became the center of family life. Sometimes it happened that a kindly neighbour would present us with a little pig, lamb, or even a calf, born prematurely when it was still very cold. The little creature could only be kept alive by the stove. So stakes would be driven into the clay floor, a little enclosure built, and another member added to the family. A deep sense of community sometimes developed between the children and the animals, so that when the time came for their sacrifice, our lives were touched with grief.

Another vision of life in a clay hut would come back to me sometimes when my own children did not want to operate the vacuum cleaner. The floors of our hut, being made of clay, would become pulverized from the impact of many feet. Often, usually on a Saturday, mother performed an operation which was the ancient equivalent of the vacuum cleaner. After sending the children to one end of the house, she would make a thin slush out of clay, and spread this mixture by hand over the unoccupied floor. Then, when it had dried, she spread a bit of straw over it to protect it. Then the children would be returned to the restored side, while she repeated the operation at the other side of the floor. This ordeal usually took a number of hours.

Another procedure needs to be described for a society glutted with labour-saving devices. Mother would sit astride a plank in a flowing stream to wash the family clothes. When soap was unobtainable she would use ashes to soften the water. In addition to caring for an ever-expanding family, mother did most of the spinning and tailoring, and spent endless nights darning and patching to cover our nakedness.

The people who surrounded us in the village and on the steppes were an interesting variety of racial and cultural fragments. There were Tartars, Kirgizen, Kazacks, Bachkirs, and a few Germans, who spoke a "low" German dialect. Illiteracy among the native peoples was almost total. Sometimes, returning late from our distant garden plot, we passed the campfires of the nomadic Tartars, a people without a written language, passing on the tales of heroism of their ancestors by oral transmission, just as some of the tales of the Old Testament had been transmitted orally for a thousand years before anything was ever written down. But getting back to the Tartars, what fascinated us children most about them were their shaggy little ponies, especially when they were engaged in wolf hunts.

Life was cruel and hard for most of the village people. Their children could be cruel, especially toward those who were different. Since our family was the only one in the village which spoke "high" German, we were immediately set apart as those who spoke "like the Bible," and were obvious targets for cruel "sports." This made it risky for us to go beyond the shadow of our house; when we sometimes did, we were at the mercy of the local hooligans. Erich was an ardent fisherman. Since fish hooks and lines were not available to us, he devised other means of catching fish. He was afraid to go alone to the stream beyond the village, so he sometimes persuaded Erwin and me to go with him. One day, before we realized what was happening, our path to the village was blocked by a gang of boys. My brothers managed to escape, but I was caught, dragged back into the river, turned face down in the water, and sat upon until they thought I was dead. By the time father arrived, summoned by my brothers, I was unconscious. With some effort he managed to revive me. The impact of this experience, as many others, was to have far-reaching consequences in my life.

But even under these harsh and primitive conditions, life was not without its thrills for the children of the exiles. Since the days in Siberia are just as long as anywhere else, and there were no ready-made toys, whatever we did to fill the hours of each day after chores were done we had to invent. Also, much of this had to be done while our parents were away from home.

My father had managed to carry, on the long trip from Poland, the family Bible, a hymn book, and a big volume on world history. Most remarkably, he had been able to hide from frequent confiscations by officials, petty and otherwise, a kit of homeopathic medicines of German origin. Along with this there was a medical book. In the middle of this book there was a two-page illustration of the human body, including a skeleton. This picture of a skeleton was something which brother Erich feared and held in dread. This gave us a powerful tool with which to restrict his freedom, or to drive him out of the house or even the village. All we had to do was open the book at the appropriate page and approach him and he did the rest. He would flee as fast as his legs could carry him, to escape this symbol of death. Only the danger of local urchins, who had no fear of skeletons or anything else, prevented us from carrying our evil deed to greater extremes.

Another adventure, which must have provided a real test of our capacity for survival, was to see how many times we could run around our house naked at temperatures of forty to fifty degrees below zero. This, too, had to be done when our parents were not home, and would only be undertaken by Erwin and myself on a moonlit night. We would run until our bodies tingled. Then we would return to the house, jump into bed, and cling to each other until our bodies regained their natural warmth. The accompanying emotions provided an unusual experience.

What greatly contributed to our survival was the system of homeopathic medicine referred to above. The system is based on principles discovered by a German physician a century or so ago. In the box were numerous little brown bottles containing various simple medicines. With the kit came a book listing the various human symptoms or disorders for each of which there was a number designating the bottle of pills to be used. For us children the significant fact was that some, or perhaps all, of these pills were sweet. Since we rarely if ever had sugar and had to satisfy our craving for sweets, typically, by sucking on the root of some prairie bush, we children broke into the box a few times to have a taste of the sweet pills. As nothing happened to us as a consequence, it led to skepticism of father's theories.

It was different with the people of the village. Since there were no doctors, the rumours soon spread that Emil Bonikowsky had magical powers and could perform miracles with his white pills. The more primitive the patient, it seemed to us, the greater the faith in my father's ability to heal. They came with every variety of ailment. Father, who had no medical knowledge except the general descriptions in his medical book, mixed his ministrations with prayer, love and pills, and sometimes seemed to perform miracles. Many people were healed. Father made no charge for his services, except to say that if the medicine should prove helpful, he hoped that they would remember our family. They usually did, and sometimes at great sacrifice. I still remember one of the Tartars coming to our door on a cold wintry morning and presenting father with a beautiful white cone of frozen milk, in appreciation for what father had done for his little, slant-eyed daughter. The milk had been saved from his own family's needs, and came either from a goat, a horse, a camel or a cow. Each day he had poured a little milk into a container, freezing it instantly, until he had sufficient to represent the extent of his gratitude. Father, in his turn, accepted it gratefully. He placed it on the edge of the roof, and whenever life in the hut became critical, a portion of milk would be chopped off, and, mixed with buckwheat, would provide kasha for another day.

Winters were not foretold with a gorgeous display of fall colour, since there were very few trees. Winter, instead, started abruptly with a howling snowstorm, which could last for days. This happened at the beginning of October, and winter lasted until the end of March, when spring and summer would arrive as suddenly as the explosion of winter. But in winter, temperatures plunged suddenly with little relief for the months to follow. In some places in this vast expanse, more than twice the size of the United States, permafrost has been found as deep as sixteen hundred feet. In retrospect, I feel grateful that there were no thermometers, so that we really never knew how cold it was. It seems to me that much of our anxiety, fear, nervousness, and even suffering, are the result of the instruments we have to measure almost everything. We measure the speed at which we travel; we figure time down to the minute and second; and we know our heart rate, our blood pressure and our weight. If we did not know all these details, we might go about our daily business with much less anxiety, more courage, and enjoy life more. This is one of the many prices we pay for living in an industrialized society. It was not until many years later that I learned that the temperature in Siberia drops to forty, fifty, and sixty degrees below zero. In Siberia we did not know this. But we did know it was not uncommon for people to freeze to death, or that parts of them sometimes had to be thawed out, as in the case of my brother Erwin once. But generally people learned to survive. In felt boots, fur caps, and layer upon layer of coats, they may have looked grotesque but they managed to stay alive.

During snowstorms all the furies of nature seemed to be turned loose, and woe to the person who found himself far away from home and from shelter at such a time. Snow seemed to come from everywhere, the earth as well as the sky. The first time our family experienced this, it seemed impossible that our little village would survive. Churning over thousands of miles of steppes, villages are the only obstructions and feel the full brunt of nature. One of these events stands out in my memory. It had been blowing for days and nights. At first we had gone out to watch the tumbling and raging snow flakes, but it soon became evident that our survival could be at stake. We locked our door, closed every crack, and listened to the fury outside. In the morning, Father, who was always the first one up to build a fire for the family, had the experience that the fire would not light, and that what little smoke there was kept coming back into the kitchen. He tried to open the door, but to no avail. He decided to wait until the sun rose, but there was no sign of it. Slowly Father realized that one of the legendary tales had become reality. Our house had disappeared, buried under tons of snow. It was not just our house, but the whole village. Not a chimney was visible — Fjedorofka was just a bit of a hump in the vast ocean of glistening snow. After this realization sunk in, exciting hours followed for the inhabitants buried alive. Someone managed to dig a hole to the surface. He then gave assistance to his neighbour, and in time the whole village was at work digging until every last house had been accounted for. The snow was cut into large blocks which were used to build a high wall at the corner of the village from which most storms came. For the rest of the winter the community was assured of some protection.

The long winter nights could be a source of pleasure, suspense, and sometimes, terror. Russia at that time was still a country with a vast illiterate population steeped in the darkest superstitions, which were perpetuated and embellished by vivid imagination. No matter how incredible were some of these tales, or how brutal their dimensions, this long-suffering and ghost-ridden people would readily believe anything. And it must be admitted that my parents felt quite at home in this environment. To overcome the isolation of these long winter nights, neighbours would take their spinning wheels under their arms, fill their pockets with sunflower seeds (their body's source of oil), and gather at one home or another to spin, talk, and eat sunflower seeds, all at the same time. This was an art which required considerable cultivation. These hoary tales of past glory and tragedy; accomplishment and failure; brutality and suffering; and ghostly manifestations from the nether world sometimes reached incredible dimensions.

For humanitarian reasons, perhaps, we children were usually put to bed early in the evening so that our minds and emotions would not be prematurely damaged by exposure to these nocturnal arrangements. There were four of us children at the time, all sleeping under one cover. We would lie very still until the stories began, then the bravest would be commissioned to get out of bed, open the door noiselessly for a few inches, and then return to the fold. The stories which filtered through this narrow opening were sometimes enough to paralyze us with dread.

One of the many problems for the family arising out of our primitive situation among an uprooted people was to provide an element of education for the children. During the five years of our stay in Siberia a number of attempts were made, all of which ended in failure. A few impressions remain untarnished in my memory. Teachers with any real education were unobtainable. But a few times some one would appear in the village and assure the elders that he was qualified. Without exception they were ruthless disciplinarians who knew little about pedagogy. Assignments were usually of a memorizing nature and had to be executed with Prussian exactness. If a child was unable to recite the lesson, not because it had not been learned but because the creature was so terrorized by fear, cruel forms of punishment would follow immediately. Usually the child was required to stretch out a hand and receive merciless lashes with a ruler or flexible willow branch. If, in anguish, the hand was sometimes withdrawn as the whip came down, the number of lashes would be increased. At other times the student had to lower his pants and lie face down on a bench and receive his lashes on his rear. When the supply of birch branches ran out, children had to go to the river after school to gather a new supply. I often accompanied them on their lonely journey, out of pity. Erwin, my brother, had a great deal of difficulty reciting his lessons under these conditions, and received almost daily doses of this sadism. I did not escape either. Another variation in punishment involved the use of buckwheat. These sharp triangular grains were put upon the floor; the student was required to roll up his pants and kneel on them with his bare knees. Sometimes these grains would become embedded in the flesh and we had to assist each other in extracting them after school was over. It is obvious that little, if anything, was learned under these cruel conditions. Usually these teachers did not last longer than a few weeks.

One teacher finally carried the matter of discipline too far. There was in the class a delicate and sensitive nine year old girl, who had, incidentally, become my first idol. The teacher beat her so severely on the hand that the skin broke open and turned black in a few days. An investigation was made and the teacher was promptly dismissed.

The only things I seem to be able to remember from these episodic attempts at education are a few psalms which we were required to memorize. The inconsistency between "The Lord is my shepherd, I shall not want...," and the brutality of the teachers and the proverty of life all about us I found difficult to comprehend, even as a child.

Wolves were another source of danger and excitement during those bleak years in exile. Siberia has long been known for these marauders who often rob people of their livestock, and, in times of extreme hunger during the long winters, will also attack human beings. This problem increased during the war years, when all guns had been requisitioned and the wolves were free to multiply. It was not uncommon on very cold nights to have the red, piercing eyes of a wolf glower through the window just above ground level with nothing but a pane of glass between the wolf and the little cluster of humanity inside. Coming home with father from church one night, we noticed a pack of wolves at the barn door of one of our neighbours. Our shouts soon brought others to the scene who, with whatever weapons they could find, tried to drive those starved animals back to the steppes. Father and I got so enthusiastic that we pursued them to the edge of the village, where they suddenly turned around to face us. Looking back, we realized that we were alone, that the rest had given up the chase. Making as much noise as we could, we retraced our steps and returned to the village in the shortest time possible. Upon investigation, it was found that the wolves had already eaten a hole through the barn door and killed a few sheep before we discovered them.

One unforgettable scene took place one crisp early winter morning when it was possible to see for miles over the vast sea of snow. The whole community was suddenly awakened by the beautiful alto chorus of howls produced by a large pack of wolves, walking single file down the road toward our village. The lead wolf usually serves as guide and director of the choral performance. The howl has a beautiful, melancholy alto richness about it. The pack only attacks when the leader attacks. Otherwise they may pass by a perfectly good breakfast, as happened that morning. In a short time much of the village was out on the street to watch the intense drama which was to take place on the road passing the village. While the wolves were approaching from the west in one long thread-like line, three sleds with their troikas were approaching from the east. Escape seemed impossible. As the two groups of antagonists approached each other, we saw the horses with their sleds move off the single track road into the deep snow and stop. When the leading wolf arrived at the point of the first sled, the whole line stopped. The community was holding its breath. Then slowly the line started moving again, repeating the intermittent melancholy chorus. The horses returned to the road; both they and the people had escaped another encounter with death. We were told later that three soldiers, who were guarding the bridge further east on the main road, had been less fortunate. The only evidence that remained the following morning of these three men was their guns and the part of their legs covered by their felt boots, which even the teeth of the starved canines could not penetrate.

Many stories of Russian folklore have their origins in man's struggle against wolves, who have inhabited these regions since time immemorial. One of the most popular is the story of the loyal servant who had taken the master and his family to a distant city by sleigh. On the way back they realized they were being followed by a wolf pack. The servant drove the troika as fast as he could, but the wolves were gaining on them. As they approached the sled, the servant cut one horse loose and sped on with the remaining two. Before long the wolves caught up again and the second horse had to be sacrificed. When the wolves approached for the third time, the servant handed the reins to his master with the request that the master care for his wife and children. Then he made the sign of the cross and threw himself into the pack. The master and his family escaped, and when the master returned the next day to the scene, he found nothing left of his loyal servant but a few bones.

The only successful weapon left during the war years against this menace to human life was the Cossacks on their shaggy little ponies. To observe their hunting expeditions was a thrilling experience. These wiry little animals had learned how to survive under Siberian conditions over the centuries. Equipped with a spear and a rope, the Cossacks on their ponies would take to the fields after a fresh deep snow had fallen, which made it difficult for the wolves to run. After a pack was located, a wild chase would ensue, until the rope or the spear had found its victim. Sometimes, as an ultimate and desperate act of self-preservation, the wolf would turn on the pursuing horse. But the latter had learned how to protect themselves. To prevent the wolf from jumping at its throat, the pony would put its head between its front legs, and run in pursuit, thrusting its legs at the wolf until it was crushed. If a pack of wolves should approach these ponies in the field, they would form a circle around their young, their heads toward the center. No wolf with any experience would approach a pony from the rear.

In the distant outside world, about which we knew little, World War I raged on. Only fragments of information reached our outpost of civilization. The assassination of Tsar Nicholas and his beautiful family came to our attention in a cruel way. The only object of beauty that I remember decorating the drab clay walls of our hut was a picture of the royal family, the last of the Romanoff dynasty. The picture showed the Tsar, a man of gentle disposition and admired by my father; the Tsarina with her aristocratic and classic Germanic features; the four daughters; and their son, the Grand Duke Alexis, whose hemophiliac condition had provided the opportunity for the peasant priest and sexual pervert Rasputin to rise to great influence in the Imperial Court. The portrait of the family had become an integral part of the atmosphere of our home. In peasant huts, it was often put in the corner with the ikons and shared a place with the hallowed saints. On our wall it stood alone. We had often looked at it admiringly, wondering about the luxurious life of a royal family, in comparison with our wretched existence. Father would sometimes tell us stories about the Tsar and about his service in the Tsar's army as a young man, when he had guarded the Winter Palace in St. Petersburg.

One morning father asked us to leave the house after breakfast. When we were permitted to return some time later, we noticed that one of the familiar landmarks of our cramped existence had disappeared. The picture of the Royal Family was gone. Father explained that the family had been executed, and that the new group in power, the Bolsheviks, had issued an order that the pictures of the Tsar must be destroyed. Not until later were we to learn the details of the execution. The Royal Family had been sent to Siberia, to the town of Ekaterinburg, and on the night of July 16, 1918, Yurovsky, who had been put in charge, ordered the Tsar, his wife, the children, a doctor, three servants and two dogs into a basement room and started the execution with his own pistol. A few soldiers completed the massacre. The bodies were then burned and the remains dumped into an abandoned mine. The fact that it was the Tsar whose order had banished us to Siberia had long since been forgotten. The story of his death came as a great shock to us. How could any human being destroy such a beautiful family, which for millions of Russians and for us expressed the ultimate of life on earth?

There was one family in our village whom we considered rich. They had the only two-storey building, and they had a majestic peacock, two black stallions and two dogs. How we admired the peacock which would strut for hours under a gorgeous display of colours. Nor did our admiration wane when we saw the stallions on display in the village. As the war ground on, military elements of various descriptions drifted to and fro, each plundering the people in their turn. Whenever we saw soldiers approaching, we children would inform the rich man, whose two sons would then mount the stallions and vanish down the river. But the time came when the warning could not be delivered in time, and two soldiers, with their guns in hand, requisitioned the horses and the pride of the village was never to be seen again.

One morning we were awakened by a bugle call. As people emerged from their huts, they saw a long line of cavalry approaching the village, preceded by a soldier with a red flag and a trumpet which he blew intermittently. The day before the village had been occupied by a division of the White Army of Admiral Kolchok. What ensued was unforgettable. As soon as the troop had been identified as belonging to a different command, bedlam broke loose. The White Army soldiers, who had been billeted with families, confiscated what they could and tried to escape. Since the road was already cut off, they headed out over the vast plains, many of them by foot, while others had managed to get to their horses. But the snow was too deep. Men as well as horses were soon exhausted, and provided perfect targets for the Red Army soldiers. One by one they were singled out by the bullets of the cavalry and sank into the deep snow. In a matter of hours, we had been rid of one enemy and fallen into the hands of another, and the plundering was repeated.

More and more refugees, some of them starving, continued to arrive in our village bringing information about life in the outlying regions. In some places the ravages of war, the severe climate, hunger, and spotted typhus and smallpox had decimated whole populations. While we still had enough grain to keep us from going hungry, it seemed obvious that it was just a matter of time before we would share the same fate. When the Lord's Prayer was used in our family worship, with more and more fervor we would intone, "Give us this day our daily bread..."

While we did not die, what we saw of hunger and the fear of starvation became so deeply imbedded in my soul that to the end of my life I shall never be able to sit down at an overladen table without seeing visions of my childhood. Also I am always aware of the starvation in the contemporary world. It is hunger that has driven so many societies into the arms of communism. This continues to happen while we go about investing billions in armaments, as if guns had ever been able to provide a loaf of bread for a starving people. While man is more, infinitely more than the bread-eating animal to which the materialist would like to reduce him, it must also be kept in mind that peace within the human family can never be secured as long as a portion of it is warped in body and mind by the crippling effects of hunger.

Our family owed its survival to many sources, but most of all to the reservoir of charity, compassion and good will which can be found among all suffering people, and especially in the people of Russia. They have not only been hardened by centuries of abuse and suffering, but their feelings have also been amplified by the pain they have known. It seems to me that no people, regardless of the degree of culture they attain, have a monopoly on either cruelty or compassion. The form of expression may differ, but the innate qualities are universal. There are no good or bad people, no good or bad nations. The line between good and evil always has to be drawn through the human heart.

Not long after our arrival in Siberia, father became an intinerant preacher, going from place to place to call the Christian remnants together and establish centers of worship. Among these remnants of uprooted humanity there was a great hunger for God, for the courage that comes through human fellowship, and for the hope that can be inspired through worship, prayer and song. Much of the spiritual hunger of these people, who were searching for a hope that found its inspiration in God, was nurtured by the message of the Bible. Many became professed Christians during the years that father spent among them. Father received no salary for his services. He was happy for the opportunity to serve his God and to share his faith with others. The people in turn were deeply grateful and did what they could for his family. Sometimes father was rewarded with a bit of butter, a bucket of grain or a piece of meat. Some of this had to be converted into other items needed by the family. Since selling on the open market had been forbidden, butter and other edibles had to be smuggled into the city at great risk. Sometimes peasants would bury a bag of grain or a piece of butter or some eggs in the center of a load of hay, in order to get it past the inspectors. But when this form of "subversive" activity became known, each load of hay was stopped and long steel rods were forced through it in order to examine the interior. Mother invented a form of subterfuge which proved quite successful. She would hide a few pounds of butter between her coat and her undergarments and manage to get them past the inspector. It was more difficult with eggs. Food would then be exchanged for needles, thread, a package of yeast, or a piece of cloth.

Just two more incidents that deeply disturbed my childhood, before we leave the story of Siberia. In the midst of all the universal human misery, these two events somehow made the universal personal, and left their mark upon the child's soul. One happened on a Sunday afternoon when a boy from a neighbouring village came to call on a friend in our community. On the way home he was overtaken by a gang of boys, dragged into an empty barn, and beaten mercilessly for long intervals. His screams soon became sobs, the sobs of a child at the mercy of his tormentors. Near evening he was thrown out on the street to drag himself home over the miles that separated the two villages. All the while this was going on, I stood under a window, wondering whether I would ever grow up and be able to do something about such cruelty. Now, more than half a century later, in a world dehumanized by another world war, with its gas chambers and scientific methods of destroying personality, I am still standing at the window, wondering how much longer it will be before the bestiality of humans can be transformed into an all-embracing nobility.

The other event started on a Saturday before Palm Sunday when we children gathered in a neighbour's garden to listen to the beautiful voice of his daughter, Emily Donner, who was rehearsing for a Palm Sunday performance in her church. She was the only child of the family, a radiant and talented spirit, gifted with an angelic voice. Two men called that evening at the home and demanded money. The father had to borrow some in order to satisfy their demand. They wanted still more and threatened to return. They did come back the next night, and on Palm Sunday father, mother and daughter were found murdered in their home. In their search for money, the thieves had taken the clock from the wall to ransack the inside. The clock had stopped at 12:30 in the morning. The grief that overwhelmed me was that this beautiful voice would never be heard again, snuffed out by the brutal hands of evil men forever. The fact that one of the men was finally brought to trial did not diminish my grief.

Chapter 3

THE ROAD BACK

In the midst of all these upheavals, dangers and uncertainties, five years had passed. Through it all, we had been sustained by the hope that some day the war would be over and we would be permitted to return to our little village in Poland. But what had started as a European war, became a world war. This in turn led to revolution and civil war in Russia, which engulfed us more and more in fratricide, political strife and pestilence. Smallpox came to our village and seriously affected three of our children. A large section of humanity had been uprooted, a nation had lost its moorings and seemed to be adrift. The laws and institutions that gave stability to a society, however unjust, had disintegrated. It was everyone for himself. Gangs of marauders swept over our village until there was little left to sustain us. Famine, which was eventually to engulf millions, was rapidly spreading. The mere rumour that there was grain in a distant village would start a mass migration. Many people would die in transit; those who survived often found the village empty. Wrote one who survived: "There is little to tell. We ate our bread. When that was gone we mixed our last flour with grass and weeds. When that was gone we ate dogs, cats, rats and birds. When they were gone, we ate each other; then we died."

Since all semblance of a national government had disappeared, people took matters into their own hands and tried to escape. In our village there were five German-speaking families left of the original exiled Polish community, constituting thirty-three individuals. By this time there were six children in our family. One group decided to attempt a return to Poland by wagon. These families managed to reach home in five months, after great hardship. Some who had many small children, including our own, decided to travel by rail. The men in our group bribed a station agent who promised that we would be permitted to load our families into a freight car. This car with its human cargo would carry a false label as cargo destined for Kiev in the Ukraine. Now started a round of feverish activity. What few possessions we had were soon collected. But there were many farewells to be made, not only from people in the village, but from those who had come to know and love father in distant communities. There were people to whom we owed so much for what they had done for our family during the years. Some offered to take us to the station. Many tears were shed during a final embrace. Barefooted and barely clothed, we left for the station where a freight wagon was waiting for us. The year was 1920.

The station agent kept his promise and had a car available. The only difference between this one which was to take us back and the one which had brought us to Siberia was that this one had an upper deck at each end. This made it possible to store all our belongings above and use the floor of the car for all other needs. After all had been loaded, the doors were closed and we were on our way west. When the train started there was no singing as before but there were prayers asking God to spare our lives. Every station we passed was crowded with hungry people, and the farther west we traveled, the more widespread and severe the famine seemed.

After a few days, we had to observe our car being uncoupled; it was moved to a side track and left there. Panic-stricken parents and children implored the station agent, but to no avail. To be left there would mean death. The station agent assured us that there was no way through to the west and threatened to send us back. A day later we were sent back to the previous station. Here a committee of two went daily to various station agents pleading and bargaining with them. While the delegates were gone, those in the car maintained a perpetual vigil of prayer. Days went by without results, until one day our men observed a group of station agents eating a dinner of potato peelings cooked in water. Our men returned to the car, took a greatly needed small carton of meat, and presented it to the officers. This promptly brought the desired results. Our car was once again hooked onto a west-bound freight train, and another threat to our survival had been overcome.

When we arrived at Kiev, the ancient capital of the Ukraine, we were ordered to leave the train. For days and nights we guarded our few personal possessions on the station platform while the men explored the surroundings in the hope of finding some means to continue our journey west. When this failed, we were loaded into another car and taken some fifteen miles outside of the city into a forest. Here we were left with the instruction that deeper in the forest there were some army barracks in which we could stay. We did as we were told. Here we were soon at the mercy of an unbelievable array of lice which had starved ever since the last soldier had left these quarters. Furthermore, we had little food left and there was no one in the forest to turn to for help. After two weeks of trying to find a way out, our family and the only other family still left pooled whatever could be spared and bought a wagon with a wretched team of horses so that we could move again. Those who were unable to walk were placed on top of the wagon-load and the rest of us walked, some by holding onto strings attached to the wagon.

It was near the end of October. There was already frost on the ground during the night. Since it was dangerous to ask for lodging because of the hate for Germans, who had started and lost the war, we had to sleep along the road at night. Sometimes when we awoke in the morning we found the bedding covered with frost and ice. Since we did not have feed for the horses, the men had to take turns pasturing them along the road during the night. It was along this track that two little sisters, Agnes and Frieda, died. They were too delicate for

Emil and Maria Bonikowski, Oscar Bonny's father and mother, on their wedding day in 1907 in Poland.

Photo of Oscar Bonny and two of his brothers taken in the Ukraine in 1925. Top left, Oscar, age 15; middle row, right, Erich, age 17; bottom center, Erwin, age 13.

such a life; their little bodies had become too weak for the ordeal. Father became temporarily blind and had to be led the rest of the way. Better food and rest helped him to regain his eyesight later.

We never reached the Polish border. Winter came, our food was gone, and we were too weak to continue. The other family had a brother living in the Ukraine in a German village; all efforts were now focused on reaching that village. We did reach Horstschick and the home of these relatives late one night. At first our companion was refused admission, until he who was thought to be dead was able to identify himself to his brother. When the door was opened there was a chaos of embraces, of kissing and weeping, while we children stood in the dark and watched. But what I remember most of this night was the midnight dinner of milk soup, black bread, and watermelons – all that this family, recently returned from exile, could provide. We ate and ate and ate until we fell asleep under the table. After many weeks we had had a full meal and were able to sleep under a friendly roof instead of a cold and merciless sky.

This village had also lost its minister while in exile. The villagers who had been fortunate enough to survive Siberia had, most of them, returned to their homes, and were anxious to have a minister for their church. It did not take too much persuasion for father to agree to remain for the winter. In a few days the family was able to move into the vacant parsonage, a comfortable building attached to one end of the church, and so arranged that father could step out of his study and into the pulpit. After the first breakfast in our new home there was a longer than usual *Morgenandacht*, because every one who could pray was given a chance to express his gratitude.

Chapter 4

THE UKRAINE

There was one stark piece of evidence left behind by the war which had raged through this village. A large shell had penetrated the wall of the living room, continued through another wall into the church, ripped off the entire choir section and thrown it against the back wall of the sanctuary. The church was surrounded by a fine orchard and some fifteen acres of land. These were put at our disposal during the years we lived there. The parish consisted of a central church, while in the surrounding area there were four additional stations which father had to visit once a month. The total membership consisted of some four hundred dedicated people. We were soon deeply involved in the lives of these suffering and struggling Baptists, so much so that when spring came our plan to continue our trip to Poland was given up. Much of father's time was spent in visitation; keeping the vital statistics of birth, marriage and death for the parish; and holding revival meetings which resulted in many new converts. Whatever father lacked in formal training and theological studies, his complete dedication to God, his devotion to people, his sincerity and his integrity made him a greatly loved and respected minister.

Three years later an invitation was extended to father to become the minister of another German Baptist parish in the Ukraine, larger than the one he was serving, and, as far as I remember, the largest in the Ukraine. A great struggle ensued. A special meeting was called by the deacons, at which members of the church implored father to remain. Some time later a delegation from the other parish arrived to emphasize their determination to secure father's ministry. Not knowing what choice to make, father resorted to his habitual way of making critical decisions, just as he had when he wanted God to decide whom of two young women he should marry. On a Sunday morning he asked the congregation to remain after the service. He appointed two deacons to prepare ballots, each bearing the name of one of the churches. After a period of prayer which father concluded with the petition of Jesus, "Father, not mine but thy will be done," a deacon drew one of the names. We moved to our next parish.

This second church was one of the beautiful Protestant churches of the Ukraine. It was a brick building erected a few years before the first world war. It had a shining tin roof and along its peak there were a series of multicoloured glass globes which could be seen from a long distance. Here again the church

31

was encircled within a twenty-mile radius by a number of stations, where people worshipped either in homes or small chapels. On the first Sunday of each month the entire parish would come together for worship in the central church and crowd it to the last seat. Sometimes those unable to enter would remain outside and participate in the worship service to be heard through the open windows. Once a month, the first Friday after the full moon, people from the central church and the mission stations would come together for a business meeting. They would then be able to walk home, some of them as far as fifteen miles, by the light of the moon.

There were a number of choirs and a brass band to enrich the worship service. It is here that I started singing in one of the choirs and also at this time I became a member of the church. I was thirteen and a bit short for my age, so that in the choir I had to stand on the pew to be able to see the music. I started singing tenor but in time had to drop down to bass. But I never stopped singing. Even after I became a minister myself I always sang in the choir of my church. How grateful I am for the joy and inspiration my soul has received through my participation in choral and congregational singing, hallowed by the tones of the organ.

Sometimes I served as chauffeur for my father on his visits to the various stations. We had a beautiful brown horse, which I enjoyed driving and caring for while my father attended to his business. On one very early Sunday morning on one of these drives we saw an unusual sight. A man came running though a field of grain at great speed. For a moment we did not know what to make of it; then we saw emerging from the field a woman, no doubt his wife, carrying a threatening weapon. This was, to my recollection, perhaps the only time I saw the masculine and feminine roles reversed in Russia.

As I grew older, I was sometimes entrusted with important confidential matters on these trips. For example, some young swain would request me to ascertain what marriageable girls were available in other churches, along with information about their appearance, the size of their dowry, and the like. Sometimes I was able to help arrange the first meeting between the interested parties.

Of the six years spent under Communism in the heart of the beautiful Ukraine, "the bread basket of Russia," I will relate a few experiences which stand out in my memory. Let me first say that school memories, which should be important in these years, were not. Because the Communists realized that it would not be possible to create their vision of a new Marxist society with a nation of illiterates, there was feverish activity to find teachers and buildings in order to provide schools for the nation. Even in our community attempts were made which, however, proved as abortive as the efforts in Siberia. Erich, as the eldest, was the only child in our family to be formally educated. At the age of thirteen he graduated from the local educational program and was sent away to an academy. An able scholar, he managed to survive, with the little resources our father could provide, on one meal a day. For the children at home there was important work to do. In the summer much of the time was taken up with pasturing a few cows and sheep on a narrow strip of land which had no fences, and with assisting in the garden, the fields and the household work.

At the age of thirteen I broke my leg, an episode memorable for the way in which this emergency was handled. While playing, the rather heavy, orphaned son of a minister fell upon me and broke the upper part of my leg. Galvanized by my screams, a group of boys tried at first to carry me and then to drag me home. When that failed, I was thrown into the wagon of a farmer who was passing by. After arriving home, my screams drove my mother out of the house, while father was left to decide on the next step. There were no doctors or hospitals, but father knew of an old man, who had operated a windmill all his life, and who was rumoured to have "a feeling for bones." He was brought to my bedside as quickly as this could be done by horse and buggy. I remember him well. He was a very old man, his back badly bent and his fingers terribly gnarled from endless toil. He was also a man of few words. He simply pushed his fist through an old wooden chair, collected the splinters, tore a bedsheet to shreds and began to attach splints to my broken leg. By this time mother had re-entered the house. She insisted that the broken leg be measured against the other leg. It was found that the bones had telescoped leaving the broken leg considerably shorter. By this time a sufficient number of neighbours who were willing to hold me down had responded to my screams. The old man took hold of my leg, braced his knee against the end of the bed and started stretching. After every one was satisfied that the two legs were of the same length, the old man left with the instruction that alcohol had to be poured on the wrapping every few hours until the healing was complete. There followed a long and interesting conflict between my inherited family ethics and the sinful proclivity of human flesh in the presence of a full bottle of alcohol. For hours I was left alone with nothing but a bottle of pure alcohol as my silent companion. When the time came I would pour the required amount on my leg. The whole room came to be filled with the aroma. There came times when I almost yielded to the temptation of having a taste of it, to find out what it was that wrecked the lives of so many people so that they sacrificed family, fortune and health. But family discipline and the fear that, having tasted the forbidden fruit once it might set into motion a chain of events I could not stop, kept me from tasting the enticing nectar. To this day I have yet to taste the first drop.

There were other times when the question of vodka presented moral difficulties for me. Sometimes people would travel long distances to be married by my father. In the winter it would be my responsibility to care for their horses. I knew that father would not perform the ceremony for people on whom there was the slightest evidence of indulgence, or who were found to have liquor on the sled which was to provide cheer and warmth on the way home from the wedding. Hence, if I came upon a bottle while in the act of putting the horses away, the guilty party would sometimes try to persuade me to have a drink, which they hoped would influence me against allowing the matter to come to light.

This I never did, but neither did I ever become an informant, not after once witnessing a scene where no amount of pleading and tears on the part of the prospective couple would soften my father's heart. I did not want to add any more grief to a world in which there seemed to be so little reason for joy.

For entertainment and recreation we had to fall back on our own resources. We never saw factory-made toys until we reached England. When I observe the gadget-saturated environment in which our children live, I am inclined to think that we may have been more fortunate. We had to construct our own toys, invent our own games, and design and build our own instruments. Some of them took many weeks to build, such as a zither, a balalaika or a violin. Some of them never produced a single note, but that did not prevent us from trying again. Like Edison with his light bulb, we discovered many ways in which an instrument simply could not be built. The reason was not always our incompetence, but the fact that so much of the raw material needed was not available. One of the most difficult tasks I ever undertook was to build a bicycle. Once a visitor came through our village on a bicycle. When he stopped, we crowded around him, looked the strange contraption over, and simply could not imagine how a full-grown human being could balance himself on two narrow wheels. We touched it, caressed it, and tried to form a mental image of it. The moment the visitor left, I went to work. At night I would lie awake reconstructing, conceiving new possibilities, only to have them fail the next day. While the bicycle I hoped to build never saw the light of day, we sharpened our skills, and that was, perhaps, the more important thing to be gained from our efforts.

Since Erich was away at school, much of the work at home became my responsibility. At age fourteen I began to use a scythe during the haying and harvesting seasons, in an effort to take a place with the men. This was such a physical ordeal that I had great difficulty straightening out my back at night. It also bothered me to have mother need to hire a man to plow our fields. Since we had a horse, I persuaded her to have a small plow made at the blacksmith's shop, so that I could save the family that expense. But when it was delivered, I discovered that it was a full-size man's plow. As I was still quite short at that age, I had to reach up instead of down to the handle bars. This put me completely at the mercy of the horse and the rocks. Whenever the blade hit a rock, it would throw me to one side or the other. This so damaged my spine that I sometimes found it difficult to breathe. To tell mother about it would have meant that I would not be permitted to plow. So I kept my secret and received permanent damage to my back. During the winter months came threshing with a flail on the barn floor. This not only required physical strength to move and sustain the flail's work; it also involved the intricate synchronization of the action of two to four flails. The slightest mistake could result not only in a tangled mass of flails but also possibly in blows to the head.

In the winter there was usually more time to play than in the summer. For example, there was ice skating on one foot on a skate that had been made at home. The exercise, however, was good for both legs as one was used for gliding and the other for pushing. Such skating was done either on the road or on the river. The latter presented something of a hazard as people often cut holes in the ice for fishing without marking the spot. This meant that people would sometimes break through and, rumour had it, would disappear under the ice to be discovered the following spring. What gave us a special thrill was the ice carousel, a Bonikowsky invention built each winter on the large pond next to the church. When the ice was strong enough a post was driven through the ice into the ground and to this was attached a thirty-foot beam. A specially constructed sled, for one person, would be attached to the long end of the pole. A number of us would push as fast as we could on the short end and the sled would thus travel in a circle at high speed. For a variation, when our parents were not home, we would hitch our big dog and the cat to the sleigh in such a way that they could only go forward. The dog followed the cat at an incredible speed yet was never able to reach it. Meanwhile the sled and passenger were moved at a high speed. Needless to say, there were other forms of enjoyment which could only be experienced when our parents were away which, of course, limited their use somewhat.

There were long hikes through the ancient mysterious forest of the Ukraine, with their untiring fascination, especially in the fall when there was a thick covering of leaves on the floor. It was here where I learned to enjoy the woods after the years on the barren steppes of Siberia. Since then whenever I have had to live in open country I have longed for the trees, "God's great cathedrals."

These pilgrimages were always made in groups, accompanied by the singing of either German folk songs or the haunting melodies of the Russians. At other times we would sit on the forest's edge and listen to the singing of groups of Russian children transforming the woods with their melancholy tunes. Since the Baptists did not allow card-playing, drinking or dancing, we would sometimes slip away unnoticed to the barn of a Russian family where a dancing party was in progress and, through the cracks in the doors, we would feast our eyes on the wild and orgiastic dances of these energetic people.

An experience which forever ruined my enjoyment of water sports happened one spring when a group of young people dared me to make a deep dive. The river which flowed through our community had a flour mill on it and one lonely bridge across it. Sometimes in spring the bridge would be torn away by floating ice and high water. It had happened again that spring. Since there was no highway commission to put up a danger sign, people would assume the bridge was there; but instead they would drive over the bank and sometimes drown. That particular spring a team of horses and a load full of people had disappeared one night. When morning came only one man was found, having been kept afloat by his heavy wooden leg! When the bridge was restored and the water was still deep, a group dared me to dive in from the bridge and return with a handful of sand from the bottom. I climbed to the top of the railing and took my plunge. On the way down I became panicky, recalling what had happened in Siberia. I felt that I was going to be crushed by the two steep shores. When I came to the surface my friends pulled me out unconscious.

The growing up process was dramatized for me by an event which in one form or another must come to most children as they step out from the shelter and supervision of the home, on their way to becoming a separate and independent personality. In our family all minor forms of misconduct were immediately punished by mother, while more serious misdemeanors were reserved for father's correction. If father was not home they were stored up in anticipation of his return. This seems like a most unfortunate procedure. In the first place, it always felt peculiar to be punished for something you had done some time ago; secondly, it always shrouded father's return, which should have been happily anticipated, in some ominous foreboding of things to come. This helped to distort the father image into an instrument of punishment rather than that of an understanding companion. But the event to which I shall refer was not one of those that could be postponed for future correction.

Mother and I were hoeing potatoes in the fall along side of each other. She was bending over her row while I was down on my knees over the next one as I tried to keep up with her. It was a windy day and I was tired and getting farther and farther behind. Suddenly the wind blew her long skirt across the path of my hoe which promptly cut right through it. When I looked up I saw a long gash in the material staring me in the face. In a country where dresses where difficult to come by, this was a calamity and no one knew this better than mother. So it is understandable that before I could take the whole situation in I saw mother's hand swinging toward my face. But the hand never reached its mark. It must have flashed through my mind that this was an accident for which I could not be held responsible. I stopped her arm. There was a brief struggle, the full implication of which neither of us could comprehend at that moment. Something had happened that would forever alter our relationship. From now on, nothing could ever be the same. There were no words spoken. We looked at each other and I assume she realized, as I did, that from now on we would have to learn to live together as two responsible individuals whose inner integrity and dignity could no longer be carelessly violated.

To return to a more mundane topic perhaps something should be said about an interesting Russian institution, the banye, which was a little bath house found behind many homes in the country. We are told that there is a clan of peasants in Russia who dip a newborn infant into cold water the moment it enters this world. This is part of the initiation the new arrival has to undergo as his introduction to life on this planet. If the child has the misfortune of being born in the winter, the ice is chopped open for this ritual. If the shock is too great or the organism is too weak to stand the test, it is fatalistically assumed that the child was not meant to live. If it survives the ritual is followed by a happy celebration because the world has been blessed with another promising occupant. In my experience the banye served a similar purpose.

One of our Russian neighbours had been trying for some time to extend to me the benefits of this institution for health and cleanliness. Rumours about what happened inside it had kept me from accepting, but one Saturday the invitation was renewed and I accepted. The banye is a small, one-room building, windowless, and usually constructed out of clay or sod. In one corner of the room is a pile of rocks which are heated to a glowing red. At the opposite end of the room are a number of shelves upon which the family reclines for the "bath." The toughest member of the clan occupies the top shelf. The ordeal usually takes place on Saturday night after the week's work is done. The stones have been heated in advance. After the family has entered the door is sealed; in this total darkness some one begins to pour water on the rocks. In an instant the room is filled with a penetrating steam. The next requirement is a thorough beating of the body with birch brooms to open the pores and sometimes even the blood vessels. Father, mother and children all join in the frolic. After the flesh has been properly softened and perspiration flows freely, the family settles down to a quiet enjoyment of the bath. Each reclines on the shelf most appropriate for his or her degree of toughness. Then comes the climax. The door is opened and each takes his turn jumping into the ice-cold water of a barrel or pool next to the banye. If this is not available the father pours buckets of cold water over himself and his family.

I regret to confess that my part in this drama was a total failure. When the steam began to build up I had no doubt that I would suffocate unless I was able to get a breath of fresh air. Since the door could not be opened, I threw myself on the floor and there, in one corner of the room, I found a tiny opening through which a bit of fresh air was seeping in from the world outside. Here I remained immovable in spite of the ridicule and promptings of my host who was having a riot of fun, screaming, shouting and laughing. If I had not found that tiny opening I very likely would not have survived that living inferno. I never again accepted an invitation of this nature, but my admiration of our neighbours increased considerably for their ability to enjoy a cleansing and rejuvenation of such dimensions.

By 1926 Communism had brought about many changes in the structure of Russian society. Lenin had been dead for two years and Stalin, in spite of Lenin's warnings about him, had ruthlessly and firmly established himself in power. While some of the structure of the new order was still in flux much of it had already been imposed with uncompromising ruthlessness and much of the outcome could already be predicted. What subsequently happened is too well-known to receive our attention here. Suffice it to say that collectivization had started and that those who stood in the way or dared to oppose the building of the "worker's paradise" were faced with imprisonment, exile or extinction. What was particularly demoralizing was the spread of espionage where neighbour would spy on neighbour or children on their parents until no one felt safe. Conversation was carried on in whispers, if at all. In the church people looked around to see who was listening. If a friend came to our house, he or she might be taken into a separate room for confidential conversation. Each one found himself surrounded by an invisible menace. There could be a knock on the door, arrest without cause or the disappearance of neighbours.

But what concerned our family and our friends most was what was beginning to happen to religion. Under Lenin people were still free to worship as they desired. Lenin had even allowed the Baptists to open a seminary in Moscow in 1921. But when he died things began to change rapidly. Marxist philosophy was used as the basis for persecution. Marx had declared that "religion is the product of the feeling of helplessness and frustration." Doing away with these debilitating experiences would result in the death of religion. He saw religion as nothing more than an opiate depriving people of the determination to change the conditions of their lives. Overwhelmed by degrading circumstances, exploited by their masters, which included the church, they were offered religion and a heaven beyond in compensation for their sufferings here below. But give them an education; place the tools of production into their hands; give them an opportunity to participate in the shaping of their destiny and there will be no need of a heaven beyond. Such was the verdict of the prophets of communism and this Russia set out to realize. It should be remembered too that much of this judgment of the church was true, especially in Russia where the church had always been a tool of the state.

The Greek Orthodox Church of Russia was morally, intellectually and spiritually a decadent institution. While one could not fail to be impressed by the solemnity of its worship service, the beauty of its liturgy, the depth of its music and the grandeur of its cathedrals, its effect upon the reconstruction of the social order was negligible. There had been a few halting attempts at reform and at education of the masses, but these were not important concerns either of the tsars or of the church. The object of these efforts was not to improve the unjust conditions of human life but to make them more tolerable. The weight of the Russian Orthodox ministry rested on irrationality, detachment from the world, and the absence of a social-moral dynamic. It was a religion without Jesus; a form of mystical worship that made no prophetic or moral demands.

The condition of the Protestant church in Russia was not much better. Here the concern was primarily with pietism and personal salvation, the avoidance of certain innocuous social practices, but not acceptance of responsibility for the social order. The primary emphasis was on "keeping yourself unspotted from the world." Hence the church was looked upon by the new order as a hindrance to scientific and social progress, which could not be tolerated. Thus, the earlier state of tolerance was soon replaced by a determination to speed the death of religion by anti-religious propaganda and active persecution of the church, rather than leave it to the slower process of raising the economic and cultural level of society, which in Marxian theory would be the outcome of collectivism.

Many methods were being used to bring about the death of the church. First came the prohibition of any religious activity outside of the church proper. Then it was decreed that the church could be used only for the purpose of worship.

Then all forms of religious instruction to minors below the age of eighteen was forbidden. Then Sunday was abolished, first by a five- and then by a six-day week. This made it difficult or impossible for families to worship together. Since the work of the clergy was not considered beneficial to the state, they were deprived of their bread cards. This reduced thousands of them to the status of beggars and social pariahs. If families were found to be providing food for a priest, they could be deprived of their bread cards in turn and food would become unobtainable for them as well. In village and monastery, in chapel and on the highway, one could see these wandering spectres, without status in the new society, their garments torn and their bodies emaciated. Many were sent into exile, others died in prison and still others met death by execution.

But there was one inevitably destructive means used against church property which made the demise of the church inevitable. This tool was gradual economic strangulation through excessive taxation. Sometimes taxes were increased weekly. The Protestant churches managed to maintain themselves a bit longer because they were supported by personal gifts. But the Orthodox church was in a worse plight because it was historically a State church and had no independent means of support. The vast Orthodox properties had all been nationalized. The Protestant churches remained open as long as there was any possibility of raising the ever-increasing assessments.

In spite of all these unrelenting efforts to stifle the churches, or perhaps because of it, father's churches continued to grow until there was standing room only. But then something happened that made father realize that the days of service to his people were inevitably numbered. By this time, some of the parishioners had already sold some of their property to make funds available for the increasing taxes on the church. Then, one day when father was away, officers arrived and informed mother that she would have to raise a large sum within twenty-four hours or the doors of the church would be locked. Mother went from door to door among the homes of the local parish. When this was not enough she went to the mission stations. Before the time had expired she had secured the demanded amount. Father knew that, though we had escaped once more, there would be another call and another until the people had reached their limits and the regime achieved its objective. Furthermore, Erich was now eighteen years old and would soon be required to enlist; I was not far behind. And if father persisted in his ministry, a return to Siberia or worse seemed a real possibility.

It was into this hopeless situation that the word America was dropped again. The word which had first reached us in Poland had, during the years of misfortune, disappeared from my memory. There had been a brief flicker of it in 1921 when a number of large green boxes arrived in our village from the German Baptists of North America. They contained second-hand clothing and a bolt of new cloth for the minister's family. How much these gifts meant to the impoverished people of the parish! Years later in another world war and its aftermath I was in charge of a city-wide clothing drive in Cleveland, Ohio for the destitute people of Europe. When it was difficult for people to see what these simple contributions on Americans' part meant to those who had lost everything, I tried to inspire them with stories of my experience in the distant Ukraine. I told them how I stood in line with the rest of the parishioners on a cold, rainy day. I hoped that there would be something left by the time my turn came at the tables. One of the reasons why charity may become difficult and joyless for givers is that it is hard for them to imagine the effect of their efforts upon the recipients. Having once stood at the receiving end, I made sure that in my churches throughout my years of ministry, there was always a large box waiting for contributions for those who had less.

Now a letter arrived from Dr. William Kuhn of Chicago, the General Secretary of the German Baptists of North America. This was now 1926. The letter informed us that an agreement had been worked out with the Canadian Pacific Railway Company and a steamship line to give assistance to those of our denomination who would like to try to get out of Russia and settle in Canada. Steamship tickets would be provided for those who could leave. I do not know how many times the letter was read. Neighbours were called in and the excitement spread. It sounded like some metaphysical abstraction, some Shangri-La existing in outer space, far removed from the world in which we lived. No one seemed to have any reliable knowledge of the country. But what father said to me when I asked him what America was like I have never forgotten: "In America you can eat white bread whenever you are hungry," he said. "In America everyone can go to school; and in America you can go to church without having to be afraid." I usually eat wholewheat bread now, but at that time it sounded like a promise of the Kingdom of God.

Father called a church meeting and read the letter from Dr. Kuhn to the congregation. Thirty-five families declared their desire to leave the country, if permission could be secured. A secretary was apppointed to register the names of those wishing to leave and to record any other important information. The next and crucial matter was that of finding a way out of Russia. The problem of securing the necessary papers proved stupendous. The bureaucratic red tape was unbelievably complex. While permission to leave could still be secured under certain conditions, many who started the process gave it up as futile. Those who persisted appointed a representative who spent weeks going from office to office until every detail had been worked out. In the case of our family, which now consisted of twelve members, it was necessary to forge some of the documents needed in order to secure the exit permit. Then with that ac-complished Father had to borrow a large sum of money as the promised passage tickets did not arrive in time from America. Fortunately one of the familiies had more money than they were allowed to take out of the country legally, and were glad to loan the excess to a reliable person.

With all the details in hand, the entire church came together for a final service of farewell. After many prayers, best wishes, and much hymn-singing, there was hardly a cheek which remained dry in that vast audience. A friend gave Father a ten-dollar gold piece. This was promptly sewn into my jacket for safekeeping until some dire need might arise. When the wagons were loaded, friends took us to the nearest railroad station forty miles away. As the village where we had spent a relatively happy part of our childhood disappeared from sight, we could still see the glistening glass spheres on the top of Father's church. When they vanished the last cord that tied us to the Ukraine was cut. We were once again adrift, in search of a distant goal and hoping for a new and better life.

It was August 30, 1926 when, for the first time in our lives, we boarded a third-class passenger car, instead of the cattle cars we had been accustomed to riding. The train took us to Moscow. There we had to report to the company doctor representing the Canadian Pacific Line for a final check-up. To the shock of our parents it was discovered that two of my brothers had trachoma, an infectious disease of the eyes. The doctor required that we remain in Moscow until the condition had cleared up. We were well aware that there was danger in any kind of delay; some government official might change his mind and, in spite of all the work already done, refuse us exit from the country. We watched the other families in our group continue on their way; our family must remain behind. Father was able to secure a one-room apartment in a basement, from which each day he walked with the children to the doctor's office for their treatment.

For me personally this was not entirely a tragedy. Since we had never been in a large city, this misfortune provided a first opportunity to observe life in a great metropolis. Moscow, by Russian standards, was a beautiful city; today it is such a one by the standards of any nation. Since we were entirely free, we spent our time walking about and visiting places which were open to us. There was the unsurpassed architecture of St. Basil's. There were the enormous arcades with their seventeen acres of floor space and exhibiting objects we did not know existed. There was the Moscow River flowing through the heart of the city; Red Square; the Opera House; the Lenin Museum; and the constant traffic of cars.

An object which stirred our imagination, indeed which seemed a miracle, was the electric light bulb that hung from the ceiling of our room. How could a glass bubble without wick or oil provide light? We soon discovered that by unscrewing the bulb, one of us placing a finger in the socket, and the rest of us holding hands, we could make a strange vibration pass through our bodies. If the last person in the chain pointed a finger at anyone's face, sparks could be seen to jump across the space toward the face. No one could explain this mystery to us. To ask was to receive stares. Father did not know either for he had never seen a light bulb. How many hours we spent pressing our faces against the store windows to observe the results of twentieth century civilization of which we had no knowledge. There were also the pastry windows and those of smoked sausage which made our mouths water, long before we knew anything of Pavlov's dogs with their conditioned reflexes.

We watched the droves of naked children in the streets and in all the alleys. It was already cold at night; we saw them lying in the ashes under the tar kettles used for road repairs in order to stay warm. There the ground was still warm. When winter came many of them would freeze to death. Later I learned more about them when I read a book about them written by Lenin's widow. She said that they numbered in the tens of thousands. She thought that many of them were the result of free love in a proletarian society. Many were orphans and others were products of an impoverished society in which parents were unable to feed their children. They were organized for survival, but even so, many of them did not survive. To get food they victimized the old women vendors who sold their products along the sidewalks. A little urchin would appear out of the crowd and take something from the display table — a piece of bread, a sausage or herring, or an apple. The woman would scream and try to rescue what had been taken. Failing, she would turn around only to find her little stand wiped clean. The police would try to be helpful but there were too many of these marauders. In time the government was able to establish homes for these children and prepare them for useful citizenship.

There was also the immense Red Square with its loudspeakers where convinced orators would make their speeches at night to anyone who wanted to listen. What impressed and fascinated me more than the speeches were the big black horns. How was it possible for them to take the human voice and spread it all over so large an area? By experimenting a little, I soon discovered that there was a place between the two speakers, far removed from the man making the address, where the sound merged. By moving the head to one side or the other, even by the smallest trifle, only one of the horns could be heard. I did not know the explanation. It belonged to a world about which I knew nothing. Only years later would I find answers to such mysteries.

One day something even more impressive happened. I had returned to Red Square where I came upon a long line of human beings standing two abreast. When I asked one of them why they were there he told me that they were waiting for the doors to open into the mausoleum where they would be able to see Lenin in his tomb. I was not sure who Lenin was but it impressed me that so many people would stand in line to see a dead man. It seemed to be more than a family funeral. I decided to join them. When the doors opened we began to move very slowly in the direction of the tomb. When I finally entered I walked down a spiral stairway into the lower regions where the body lay. The utter silence, the mysterious illumination and the soldiers with fixed bayonets at every turn of the stairway, filled me with something approaching terror. I finally reached the death chamber where the well-preserved body of the first great revolutionary leader of communism lay enshrined in a glass pyramid. A black velvet pall was drawn over his chest, his head was on a dark satin pillow, and his hands lay at his sides. All of this in the glow of an eerie illumination left an unforgettable impression. I had been so frightened on my first visit that I went back a number of times to verify what I had seen. We are told that the tomb was erected at the spot outside the Kremlin Wall where Ivan the Terrible is supposed to have had an opening from which he could watch the torture and execution of his enemies and, sometimes, his friends.

Many times I stood on the long ramp leading through one of the towers of the Kremlin Wall into the interior. I had no idea what was confined within these walls. Of course, I could see some of the buildings looming above the walls, especially the gold-covered church domes. We had been told that it contained the largest bell in the world, which had fallen to the ground when the church tower for which it was cast collapsed under its weight. The piece that broke out of the bell when it hit the ground was supposed to be big enough to allow a team of horses and a wagon to drive in and out. This and other stories made me determined to see the interior. One day I attached myself to a wagon, walking close behind the driver in the hope I would be taken for his son. What I had failed to notice were the two soldiers with weapons, hidden in niches on each side of the tower gate. As the wagon passed through the gate, the two soldiers stepped out. In terror I took to my heels down the ramp and into the tall grass along the shore of the Moscow River where I hid until I could safely return to the road.

During all this time, Father was faithfully going to the doctor each day, leading the two little boys by their hands. Weeks later he was informed that the conditions had been corrected and that we could now resume our journey. Before leaving Moscow we had been duly warned by an agent of the Canadian company to be very careful in our conversation with strangers on the train until we had crossed the border into Latvia, then an independent country. One slight mistake could be enough to terminate our exit. As we got on the train it soon became evident that all passengers were under close surveillance by agents of the government. At the border the luggage was carefully examined and all papers were checked. One inspector took possession of father's meager collection of books, wrapped them in his jacket and made for the door. However, father had secured a special permit for his books. When he produced this document, the "inspector" dropped the books and vanished.

Slowly the train moved across the border. When it stopped on the other side, the Russians disappeared and the Latvian officials took over. What a relief this was. Here we could finally breathe freely. One no longer had to look upon any stranger as a potential enemy or spy. To be treated as civilized human beings by officers who were clean, courteous and neatly dressed, instead of the familiar shouting, cursing and bullying of the Russian proletariat! We simply wept for joy.

When we arrived at Riga, the capital of one of the most advanced republics of the Baltic states, we experienced treatment which must have been refined through many years of contact with Russian immigrants. We had the first shower bath in our lives, and, while enjoying this luxury, our clothes and our luggage were sent to an infirmary where they were thoroughly disinfected and deloused. Thus within a short space of time all that had clung to us for eleven long years, emotionally, mentally and physically, was left behind. We emerged in a fresh and beautiful new world in which every human life and even the landscape seemed to be bathed in a new glow.

But, of course, not everything was left behind. No one who has ever lived in the stifling atmosphere of totalitarianism; who has had to spend years in the shadow of the secret police; and whose life has been at the mercy of men whose brutality and passion were not accountable to a civil code of law, can ever leave his past behind. There are wounds which time, love and friendship can heal, but there are scars which can never be erased. They lie too deep for the healing hand of time. There are fears, feelings, memories and complexes which have become a part of the vast subconscious and lie beyond the reach of volition. Much of this continued to provide the material of my nightmares and dreams for years to come. But what may perhaps be even more burdensome is that some of these experiences, especially those we had during the most impressionable years of childhood, harden into character and determine our judgments, conduct and responses to the world, thus making it difficult for others to understand us. This is some of the baggage we are doomed to carry through life.

Chapter 5

THE ROAD TO CANADA

We remained in Riga for only a few days, enjoying the beauty of this wonderful ancient city with all its evidences of a much more advanced civilization than what we had known in Russia. Then we took a boat to England by way of the North Sea. The joy of that trip has remained vivid in my memory; the green fields, the well-kept roads, the well-maintained farm dwellings along the shore, and the happy, busy people we met at the ports along the way. Impressive to me beyond compare were the high-suspension bridges as we passed through the Kaiser Wilhelm Kanal. As the ship approached, some of them opened up like gates pointing toward the sky, while others opened and turned on a horizontal plane. In Danzig, where we spent one day, we were able to meet mother's sister Natalie Zozmann, who was working for a noble Polish family in that city. Here we heard for the first time the classic German language used in public. Here we were impressed by the extreme politeness of the store personnel, even when one did not buy anything. There was no arguing, no pushing, no bartering, and no insults, nothing but graciousness and courtesy.

After a rough night in the North Sea, flanked by many warning signals from the fog horns, our ship sailed up the Thames to London on October 4, 1926. Then we were put on a train for Southampton, where we were unloaded at a World War I aeroplane hangar which had been turned into an immigration and refugee center. After another medical inspection we were told that the eye infection of the two brothers had returned and that the smallest member of the family, little Harry, who was only two months old, was also sick. Then something happened which we were unable to explain and about which our questions were never answered. It had been the practice of the steamship company to retain the sick members of a family and permit the rest to go on. In our case they refused to do this, even though mother had agreed to remain with the sick children. Again we had to reconcile ourselves to an uncertain future, while the rest of the company which had landed with us boarded another ship for Canada. Father made it plain that he would not accept responsibility for the debt incurred by those members of the family who were not sick. All father's efforts to correct the situation fell on deaf ears. Other complications soon set in. Little Harry was taken to the hospital and died. Mother was hospitalized twice for breast infections. Some of the children had to be quarantined because of an epidemic of measles.

The total number of immigrants detained at Atlantic Park, a few miles from Southampton, was over four hundred. Some had been there for three years or more. One day father and a number of others were called into the administration office, where it was demanded that they make payment on the debt that was growing daily or secure a Canadian sponsor who would be willing to assure payment. All the borrowed money was now gone; there was nothing left even to make a token payment. Most of the others were not much better off. Hence they were dismissed from the office with the warning that if some payment was not made soon, all would be returned to Russia. This was such a frightening possibility that the men came together and drew up a letter to the Soviet Consul in London to ask his help and advice. He replied that no one could be returned against their will, nor would he give them visas to permit it. A copy of the letter must also have been sent to the immigration office, for in subsequent meetings that threat was never again used.

Life in time settled down to a simple routine of eating the frugal fare provided by the Atlantic authorities, sleeping and hoping. The only person in our family who would not rest concerning the injustice done to us was Erich. He managed to get some material and set about to acquire the English language as fast as he could. It took months, but when he was ready, he drew up a letter of complaint to the immigration office in London. In time an investigation was made, the previous verdict was reversed, and we were permitted to proceed on our way to Canada. But that was a year after our arrival; in the meantime, we had to find a way to fill the days and weeks with meaningful activity.

Those of us who were not quite as scholarly as Erich had to find other things to do. Some of us joined a refugee rugby team which filled some of our time with a wholesome competitive enterprise. But we wanted to be useful too; we wanted to earn something since there was not a single penny among us. On the Atlantic Park premises a lady maintained a canteen with many little niceties, such as lemonade, cakes, raisin kuchen, candy and other tempting items. As most of our meals consisted of smoked fish, boiled eggs, bread, a bit of meat at long intervals, and very strong-smelling oleo-margarine, the little canteen presented a real temptation. We had to find some way of making money on our own, for getting a job was prohibited by law. Our first attempt was to make an agreement with our cook to let us have our eggs unboiled. As soon as I could find an outlet with one of the Southampton food stores, we began to advertise among our fellow immigrants for more eggs. Soon we were able to deliver eggs on a weekly basis to the store. Since this had to be done by bicycle I was not always successful in getting them delivered without some breakage. And how much we enjoyed our first meager income, the first money we had ever had!

Then one day fate struck again. The painfully constructed enterprise collapsed. The eggs (which, of course, we badly needed in our diet) were no longer accepted at the store. This business had been carried on without the benefit of spoken language. I could not speak English and our retailer was unable to speak German, Russian or Polish! One day when I was making a delivery, our contact man refused to accept the eggs. What he tried hard to make clear to me I could not understand. I gave him a piece of paper and managed to make him understand that I wanted the reason for his refusal written down. This I showed to Erich who explained to me that the good man would not take our eggs because they were bad. Only years later did I learn that these eggs were shipped in from Norway and apparently had been on the road too long before they reached the customer. He had been losing some of his customers by selling them our eggs. I could appreciate his difficulty and certainly had no intention of ruining the good man's business. It meant that now the eggs would have to be eaten by the people for whom they were intended.

But once having tasted the satisfaction of having a bit of cash of our own, it seemed awful to consider going back to a moneyless status. We promptly looked in other directions in the hope of finding another enterprise. The answer came to us one evening while we were observing a familiar character around the Park carrying on a brisk little business of his own. He had something like a portable dime store, either suspended from his neck or resting on a little portable table. Almost every week, ships with Polish, Czech and other refugees were arriving in London. They would come to Atlantic Park by train, and there they would wait for a ship from Southampton or Liverpool to take them to Canada. They were good targets for portable merchandising.

We were soon ready again for business, starting, of course, on a very small scale as the funds for the original capital investment were tragically limited. But as business grew, we were able to expand so that before long we were doing quite nicely. The Poles had been in a fine spirit and did not mind spending their last dollar for a billfold, a pair of shoe strings, a fountain pen or a pair of stockings. Weren't they just a few days away from the gold mines of America? Then, one evening, while things were still going quite well, the arm of malice touched our lives again. I saw the officer of Atlantic Park approaching; by his face I could tell that he was up to no good. While I was trying to fold up my little businesss like the tents of the Arabs and as "silently steal away," he caught up with me. Did I have a permit? And in a language I could understand he made clear to me the conditions under which a legitimate business could be operated in England. This was not Russia, he gave me to understand. Here an enterprise, no matter how small, could only be operated with the appropriate authorization, which had its own price. Under these conditions I knew that I could not succeed; the margin of profit was too small and the volume too limited.

But I was willing to try once more. Our next and last effort to become entrepreneurs was a dramatic, enjoyable, wholesome enterprise, and one which could be operated without a permit. My younger brother Erwin and I secured a number of broken-down bicycles from a junk pile; repaired them; and in time were able to put a fleet of them in operation. Our fee was a shilling per hour. If you had never ridden a bicycle before, we could teach you. Poles, Greeks, Croatians, Yugoslavs and all the rest went wild over the opportunity to stretch their limbs after confinement in the small world aboard ship. Unfortunately only a few of them knew how to ride a bicycle. We would support them until they claimed they could take care of themselves, which was usually long before they had learned anything. We would then turn them loose, which left them at the mercy of the rough landing strips around the plane hangars or in the hangars themselves. If a cycle was broken, which was often the case, it was promptly repaired and a reasonable price charged for the damage. If a client refused to pay, we threatened him with a report to the Park commissioner. While such a report could never have been made, it usually brought the desired result. Damage to the bikes was only part of the story; the other part was bruised elbows, noses, knees and torn clothes. One day I stood by when a powerful Pole, after I had started him out, drove full speed into the wall of an airplane hangar; he hit the building with such force that part of his body went through the sheetrock wall. When I helped to extract him, he was bleeding from many wounds but the spirit of the brave man was unbroken. The bike was a total loss.

There were things to see and to enjoy in England. We never tired of the beautiful countryside with hedges, rivers, gardens, ancient chapels and the ringing of the church bells across the island at eventide. Often we bicycled over paths through fields and winding lanes, meadows and rolling hills, returning at the close of day tired but grateful for our freedom and for the ever-changing beauty of nature and the friendly people on this pleasant island. In Southampton we watched the great giants of the ocean being lifted out of the water for painting and renovation. In the little town of Isley we worshipped a number of times with a small group of Christians, a most friendly people. While we could not speak their language, we could join them in the singing of familiar hymns, they in English and we in German. We enjoyed their cordiality and the warmth of their fellowship.

In 1927 we were informed that the healthy portion of the family would be permitted to leave for Canada. Helmut, eleven, and Arthur, six, were unable to qualify because of their eye condition. Since they were too young to remain alone, my sister Alma, who was fifteen, remained with them. On May 14, 1927 we boarded the Empress of Scotland, a former German liner which had been taken by England as part of the reparations after the first World War. While Lindbergh was making history by crossing the Atlantic toward France in the Spirit of St. Louis, our boat was on its way to the new world, the land of the brave and the home of the free.

We arrived in Quebec on May 23, 1927. After our papers had been checked, we took a train to Winnipeg, Manitoba. There we were welcomed by a group of German Baptists who had made our trip from Russia possible. After a day of good eating and much visiting, we departed for the little community of Esk, Saskatchewan, where father was to take charge of a small Baptist church. Here Alma and little brother Arthur joined us a year later, and after a second year, Helmut also arrived.

Although it was already the end of May, there were still high snowdrifts in many places. The town of Esk, which we saw as we emerged from the train, consisted of a grain elevator; a grocery store and post office combined; a hardware store; a drug store; and a creamery station. Father's church was a very small structure a little distance from town. The parsonage was primitive and run-down, a place which had been used to house other refugees. After a few days, during which a group of church members did what they could to renovate the building, we were able to move in. One farmer loaned us a cow and a horse, until we would be able to buy our own. Thus we had a means of transportation and a perpetual supply of milk. For days we were taken from family to family for dinner. Some of them had known father in Russia and had managed to get to Canada before we did. As far as our meals were concerned, for a time at least, we must have lived like the Roman aristocracy shortly before the fall of the Empire.

With an astronomic debt overshadowing the family and father's salary hardly enough to take care of the most essential needs, Erich and I had to find jobs as soon as possible, in order to contribute to the family income. I was able to locate a job with a German farmer close to Esk, a most understanding and kindly person, except in one respect to which I shall refer a little later. At first I managed the work quite well, although my body was poorly equipped for hard labour at that time. Plowing, building fences, clearing away the underbrush, and caring for the farm animals were all within my physical ability. My suffering began with the start of the threshing season. This was a year in which the farmers of Saskatchewan were harvesting up to thirty bushels to the acre, which meant that each individual bundle of grain was heavy and difficult to manage. This was especially true for one who had lived for a year on English smoked herring. Because of the shortage of labour we had an inadequate crew for the size of the machine, which had to be kept going ten to twelve hours a day. There seemed to me to be no limit to the amount of grain this insatiable Moloch could devour in a day. I was the weakest link in the labour chain. Often I had to return to the separator with a load only half full, dump what I had into the separator, and hurry back to the field for another load. The other crew members were seasoned veterans who seemed to carry on without much effort, while I often reached my breaking point. At night my arms would be so swollen that I would have difficulty getting my shirt off. Since I did not have the courage to explain to the farmer that I could not go on any longer, I spent much of my time while loading the hay rack contemplating a way of escape. I had never seen a map, had no idea where I was in Canada, and certainly had no idea to where I might escape. I did not want to mention this to the parents either, since they already had enough problems of their own. My plan was that after a day's work and the dinner that followed, when I had to go to the barn to care for the horses, I would not return. Instead I would go to the railroad track, start walking, and perhaps find some work that was within my limits. Then I would let the parents know where I was. Yet every evening, during the dinner which was a tremendous meal, the farmer, who was all congeniality, would tell a few jokes, I would begin to feel better, and then lose my courage to execute the plan I had made during the day.

By the time we were through threshing, snow had already fallen and the last few days the sheaves had to be pulled out of snowdrifts. Yet, in spite of these conditions, the good man informed us that he had offered to thresh the harvest of an elderly widow who was unable to find anyone else to do the work. Stronger now, I decided it was best not to make a complaint. We moved the equipment to her farm and continued to thresh at a temperature far below zero.

It was agreed that I and my team of horses were to remain on her farm during the time we were working there. This I liked since she was a very kindly, thoughtful person who would do anything she could for us. This resulted in an experience that has never again been equaled in my life. While I was gone, one Saturday night, this dear lady had put a hotwater bottle in my bed, so that I would return to warm comfort. I had never seen or experienced a hotwater bottle before. When I crawled into bed that night and landed on the bottle, the sensation was so extraordinary that I could not imagine what I had done. I let out an inhuman scream. When the lady arrived in her nightgown, she found me standing in the middle of the room, pointing toward the bed, speechless. I was sure I had crushed an infant.

Much of the first winter, sometimes at a temperature of forty below, I spent clearing away underbrush and cutting down trees to prepare land for cultivation. My pay was room, board and one dollar a week. When the time came that spring to cultivate the virgin land which I had prepared for the breaking plow, I reached another crisis of a different nature, but one which made me think of escaping again. It took from six to eight horses to pull the mammoth breaking plow with its stump-splitting knife. In order to avoid getting stuck, when the team approached a stump or pile of roots, the horses had to be driven quickly so that the momentum would carry the plow through. One of the horses, Barney by name, a huge and awkward creature with a touch of rheumatism, laboured with great difficulty. Often when the plow hit a stump and failed to split it, the impact would cause Barney to lose his balance and fall. In spite of the beating on the part of the farmer, the poor creature was unable to rise to its feet. When everything else failed, he would tie a chain around the horse's body, hitch another horse to the chain, and pull Barney back on his feet. All of this must have caused unbelievable pain to the animal. Sometimes this cruelty used to haunt my dreams. I could not understand how a person, so thoughtful and kind otherwise, could be so cruel in the treatment of an innocent animal. Again I began to think of escape but the thought was never executed. It did, however, help me to understand why St. Paul spoke of "the whole of nature...longing for redemption."

In the meantime, the parents had moved to another church, in Lockwood, twenty miles from Esk. Since there was no parsonage here, friends advised them to purchase a farm, with buildings, near town. If all went well this could provide some additional income for the family. Again, the money had to be borrowed.

Additional horses, farm implements, and seed grain had to be purchased. The soil on this eighty-acre farm turned out to be very sandy. For three years the parents lost every bit of grain they had planted because of a sustained drought and windy conditions. Each year seed grain was purchased, only to be blown away. Erich and I contributed what we could, but it all seemed like a bottomless pit. The economic level of the family had sunk so low that often mother would do the laundry after the children had gone to bed. She would mend and darn, patch and iron during the night, so that there would be something to wear to school when day came.

Meanwhile, during the second year of the parents' farming, an opportunity came for me to go to work for a Mennonite farmer in Drake, Saskatchewan, some twenty-five miles from the parents. Mr. Bartel was a good-natured, splendid person, and his wife a wonderful mother to a brood of five children. He and his two brothers had all bought their land around their father's farm, so that they could do many things together. Here I remained for the next three years, satisfied with my new boss who was more of a companion than an employer, and pleased with the many new friends I soon had in this model Mennonite community. But here again there was no opportunity to learn English. They spoke a low German dialect which I acquired so proficiently that in a few months no one suspected me of an alien background; I had become one of them. My pay was still a dollar a week in the winter and a dollar a day in the summer. By this time I had regained my Russian hardiness, and was able to endure any amount of hard work. During the threshing season, which usually lasted over one month because the Bartel family owned a large outfit and did all of their threshing together, twenty-five men were required. We had our mobile sleeping quarters, twelve bundle teams, spike and field pitchers, and whatever else needed to keep this outfit going from morning until evening for some five or six weeks. We ate five times a day. By now I was able to hold my own against anyone, including the Poles who were usually a part of our crew each year. Together we accomplished a prodigious amount of work. I had become a man among men, could pit my strength against any of them and I had gained their respect. I enjoyed my work so much that sometimes when I was working with the horses in the field, I was reluctant to come home at night. Bartel told me one day, "Oscar, I don't care what you do to yourself, but for heaven's sake, save my horses."

There was a little white church in the community to which all the Mennonites went each Sunday to worship. They did not believe in a trained ministry. A respected elder of the community who was known for his integrity, his charity and a good life would preside at the worship service. I sang in the choir, attended a youth discussion group, and very much enjoyed this lay religion in which there was no occasion for theological strife, Biblical fanaticism, noisy revival meetings, or factional tension.

When the week's work was done, a number of young men would usually come to our farm on Saturday night, when, after cutting each other's hair, we would go to town for the evening. After promenading up and down Main Street, speaking to a few farmers or their children, we would end up in the Chinese restaurant, the only eating place in town. We would each have a cup of coffee and a piece of "boughten" pie (in contrast to the home-made pie served regularly at the Bartel home). Sometimes we managed a date with one of the fine Mennonite girls and then would turn homeward again to rest and be in church the next morning.

Sunday nights were equally happy occasions. We would meet in one of the homes, where we talked, provided our own instrumental music, sang, played games, and enjoyed coffee and cake. When we took our dates home, there could be the holding of hands, sometimes a shy kiss, and the promise to see each other again soon. Monday morning found us again at our jobs for the rest of the week, except for Wednesday night when we had choir rehearsal. What was especially beautiful in the winter was to climb into a big bobsled, as many as could be packed in, and drive out into a glistening moonlit night, singing the folk songs, at that time in vogue in Canada, in four-part harmony. How clean and wholesome this life still seems to me after living for years in congested cities, where the corner drugstore, the saloon or bar, and the theater have replaced the warmth and intimacy of the home, the open air, the intimate fellowship and the community skating rink.

Every town of any size had its outdoor skating rink, or if large enough, one housed in a Quonset-type building. This was the Canadian equivalent of the American bowling alley. Since the winters were long, there would usually be four months of ice at least. By now I was able to enjoy not one hand-made skate but two factory-made ones.

One winter I attended a Bible School held for a number of weeks in one of the Baptist churches in Nokomis. The program consisted of instruction, discussion, Bible reading, singing and a time for recreation. It was here that I met Olga, who made a deep impression on me. She came from a fine family and had even more than the usual amount of feminine charm. With the aid of a mutual friend, we managed to arrange a date and did some skating together. But as was my misfortune during those years in Canada and later in the United States, I found it difficult to carry on a conversation when I found myself alone with another person, especially if that person was a woman and if that woman was especially attractive. I suffered from a childhood timidity, self-consciousness and a sense of inferiority. I could hold my own in a group very well and sometimes even become the life of the party, but, individually, face to face, I had a difficult time. Hence I had to avoid situations where I would have to face Olga alone. So we attended social gatherings and went skating together. She was a fine skater, a gracious partner and provided a real thrill for me on the rink, especially on nights when the high school band was playing and the whole town was there in gay winter colours.

But the Bible School was ending, summer was coming, and I did not have the means of travelling the distance that separated us. So the star that had risen so full of promise on my social horizon was gradually setting. However there were other fine friendships which contributed to the slow and painful evolution of the social self. Here I will speak only of one other relationship which took me to the most important turning point in my life.

We will call her Gretchen, a name taken from the beautiful and idyllic episode in the life of the German poet Goethe which, for him, too, ended in tragic disappointment. But it left an unforgettable mark upon him. Near the end of his life he immortalized her in the beautiful child-like creature Gretchen in Faust. When I met my Gretchen she was in the last year of high school. She played the violin and, with her sister and father, was a member of a small family ensemble. She was a child of great friendliness; a gentle spirit, sensitive to every form of human pain; tolerant; sympathetic; and a bright student. The family, of German origin, was of modest means. The parents had educational limitations, but they maintained a cheerful home which was a rallying point for many of the young people in the area. In a year Gretchen was to graduate from high school as the valedictorian of her class. I had met her many times at social gatherings with the group which both of us frequented. Refusing to go steady with anyone, she was a cheerful companion for many.

I became thoroughly obsessed with Gretchen, so that as the months wore on I reached a point of desperation. I remember a time when both of us attended a party in another town. It was a dreadfully cold night, and her cousin was driving us in a very old car without a heater. When he reached his home near midnight, he refused to go any further and we had to agree to spend the night at his home. When I awoke early next morning and left my room, I noticed Gretchen and her sister sleeping beyond a glass door. For a long time I stood, door knob in hand, looking at her, a picture of beauty and innocence, and debating whether I should place a kiss on the lips of this sleeping beauty. As so many times before, courage left me, and I passed on down the stairs.

But time was running out; I knew that I could not go on like this much longer. A day or so later I saw a glimmer of hope in the advertisement of a book in a German-Canadian newspaper. It was entitled *Die Kunst der Gewandten Unterhaltung*, The Art of Fluent Conversation. It said in very fine print that anyone familiar with the contents of this book would be able to carry on a fluent conversation on any subject, at any time and under any circumstances. This seemed to be promising a great deal, but I was desperate and not in the mood to ask any questions. I ordered it, read it as best I could by spelling out each word, repeating it a number of times and committing some of it to memory. Then I felt I might have a better chance at our next encounter. It so happened that it fell to my lot to take Gretchen and a number of other young people home the following Sunday night. After the rest of them had been delivered home by buggy, the situation seemed propitious. Yet when I stopped the horse in front of her house, I could not remember a single line from the good book which had promised so much. We said goodnight, and as I was driving home I felt disgraced.

By this time I had reached a point of no return. I persuaded a friend to write a letter of proposal for me. I kept it for days while trying to get up enough courage to mail it, but I feared that it might extinguish the little flame that had been so painfully nurtured. I finally mailed it, and could not eat for a few days or sleep for a few nights, as I waited and hoped for a reply. In time it came. When I opened it, I found it to be a document in her lovely hand-writing and in the Gretchen spirit. She was very appreciative of our friendship, and not wanting to hurt me for anything, but ended in the tragic refrain that she could not marry me.

This was such a blow, which, added to all the past disappointments and dangers in my life, left me completely dazed. As the reality gradually began to sink in, I began to brood over it. I read the letter again and again for any possible element of hope. When none came I slipped into a depression which, in time, took on an element of irrationality. As every human being has his breaking point, I seemed to have reached mine. Not even my closest friends were able to reach me with anything helpful. During one of my agonizing, endless, sleepless nights, the idea of suicide presented itself to my reeling mind. At first I rejected it, but it kept on returning with stronger and stronger persistence until it seemed the only way out. As day was breaking I found myself on the way to the woods with my rifle. But before the act could be carried out, I was startled by a sunrise. Confronted with the possibility of a new day, my courage left me.

The original plan having failed, a solution had to be found in another direction. Finding it impossible to see her again, I tried to find out through a mutual friend why she had turned me down. The reason she gave was that I was illiterate. I did not even know the meaning of the word and had to ask what it meant. It is difficult for me to understand now how I could have grown to the age of twenty-one without ever realizing that I had no formal education, that I was ignorant and that I should try to find a way to get at least some education.

Of course, during the earlier years life had been so full of events, dangers and excitement that education could easily be overlooked. In Russia I had been one of the eighty-five per cent who could neither read nor write, and there was little reason to miss it in such an environment. In Canada I soon had many friends who loved and respected me, and who must have overlooked this lack in me. I enjoyed physical labour and the wholesome life on the farm, and the people for whom I worked were impressed by my zest and satisfied with my achievements. Now and then I would hear people discussing things I knew absolutely nothing about, but that apparently was not enough to awaken the soul and send me on a search for richer fulfillment. These circumstances made the present blow even more devastating. However, instead of cursing like Hamlet the day that brought me into the world, or the circumstances of history that robbed me of a normal childhood, I resolved to find a different answer. Never again was a woman to turn me down because I was illiterate!

My parents by now were completely bankrupt. Three crop failures had not only wiped out whatever little they had, but they were helplessly in debt.

Whatever I was able to earn I had sent home, but this was not enough to save them. Erich had long since left the farm and gone to Rochester, New York to study. I decided to quit my work with the Bartels and return home to see if I could help the parents save their farm. To make the effort worthwhile, I rented an additional farm. I had the hope that with more acreage we could substantially improve our situation. In the meantime, I sought out and made a friend of the high school principal, who allowed me to sit in the back of the room during school hours in the winter months. I was curious to know just what happened in a classroom. But this proved useless, since I did not know what the titles of the textbooks meant, let alone benefit from the class discussion and instruction. I tried attending a grade school, but the children laughed at me. From home and friends there was also no encouragement. They could not understand why I was so concerned about education. Wasn't I doing as well, if not better than most? I was elected president of the youth organization in father's church. I believe I made a few speeches and even participated in a debate. Today I cannot remember what the topics were or who won the debate. However, the question of illiteracy could not be dismissed or silenced. Something had stirred my soul into a new awareness in a way in which I had not been touched before.

There was in existence at that time in Rochester a German Baptist Academy and Seminary on the European pattern. The academy provided a four-year course of study which consisted of the last two years of high school and the first two years of college. Upon graduation from the academy a student could enter a three-year seminary course and graduate with a theological diploma which qualified him for the ministry of any of the German Baptist churches then prevalent through the United States and Canada. My brother Erich, after trying it on a farm in Canada, realized, as did his boss, that he was unsuited to physical labour. Sometimes he would pick up a sheaf of grain, be struck by an idea, and simply stop in the middle of a field to pursue its ramifications. So he returned to his first love which was learning. He was the only one of our family's children who had had formal education in Russia; the parents, at considerable sacrifice, had sent him off to one of the Tsar's schools. With his basic education, in England he had learned to read and write English. So he had readily gained admission to the Academy at Rochester about three years earlier, before I reached this crisis in my life.

Since there was no other place to which I could turn, I began to focus on that academy, where they were at least using German, the language I spoke, as the major language. I turned to Erich for help, begging him to intercede for me with the school administration. He knew me too well and tried to talk me out of it. I again turned to a friend who helped me compose and write a letter to the Dean of the school informing him of my determination to get an education.

Anxious weeks followed until a reply arrived in which the Dean informed me that in the many years of the history of the institution they had made many exceptions, but that they had never had a case like mine. Indeed, he said that I should not come. Meanwhile my year of farming was a total loss; neither the parents nor I was able to harvest anything, because of the poverty of the soil and a terrible drought. The money was all gone; every dollar of mine had vanished in the parched fields which refused to reward our efforts.

This left me with nothing but my determination to become an educated person. Fall was approaching and time was running out. I had to come to a decision. I resolved to borrow the necessary money for a ticket to Rochester, to arrive at the school on the fifteenth of September, when the fall semester began. I would confront the faculty and beg them to allow me to stay for one year.

There were just two more experiences that deserve mention before we leave Canada. One happened when I arrived in Regina and the American Consulate demanded a paper that verified my legal entry into Canada. This made it necessary to call my parents long distance. I had never made such a call. I have forgotten how many times I walked into the telephone booth, took off the receiver, hung up and walked away with perspiration rolling down my face on a cold day. When, years later, I watched my little six-year old daughter take off the receiver ready to dial almost anywhere in the universe, I could not help recalling my predicament in Regina when I was twenty-one. The trauma of that first long distance call has remained with me; I have never learned to use and enjoy the telephone with abandon. But I must have made the call; in a few days the necessary papers arrived and I was able to secure a visa.

The other experience happened in Winnipeg, Manitoba. A young man whom I had recently met and who was a recent arrival from Germany and a graduate of an academy there, joined me on the way to Rochester. Karl Korella and I arrived in Winnipeg on a Sunday morning, to learn that there was no train to the United States on Sunday. Karl was also a person of very limited means. Neither of us had counted on the possibility that we might have to spend an extra day on the road. We spent the day walking around and seeing the city. By evening we had become quite hungry. Because we could not afford a restaurant, we purchased a can of pork and beans and a loaf of bread. Then we walked to beautiful Central Park in the heart of the city, where we could sit after a day of walking and fasting, to enjoy the evening meal. How could I forget that evening! Karl and I sat on a park bench under a light trying to open the can with a rock, while all around us people were promenading arm in arm or holding hands, expressing love and affection. After the can was opened, we tried to extract the contents with slices of bread. For me this was a novel experience. I had never had an encounter with a can of pork and beans before. It was natural that I should place emphasis on the pork, yet we finally reached the bottom of the can without my ever having seen or tasted a bit of meat. So there was nothing left but to question the integrity of my new friend; I assumed that he had gotten all the pork. Years later while visiting Karl in Canada I talked with him about this experience. He confessed that he had suspected me of the same thing, but was too polite to question me. I have never again put the emphasis on pork when confronted with a can of pork and beans.

Oscar Bonny and Helen Lindquist on their wedding day in Lawrence, Kansas in the fall of 1943.

Oscar and Helen Bonny and their three children at Christmas time, 1953. in Kansas City, Kansas. The Bonny children, left to right, Francis, Erich, and Beatrice.

After our one meal for the day, we took one last envious look at the romantic surroundings, and then sought a possible place to spend the night. Since we had no money for a night's lodging, we picked out an appropriate spot on the bank of the Red River which flows through the city. It was already cold and there was frost on the ground. Here we lay with nothing but our raincoats covering our bodies and God's eternal stars overhead. The next morning our bodies were stiff and our coats were covered with heavy frost, but the sun rose in full splendour and gave promise of a beautiful day. With gratitude in our hearts we divided what was left of the loaf of bread, walked back to the station and boarded a train for the United States.

Chapter 6

ROCHESTER: THE ACADEMY

Two days later Karl Korella and I arrived early in the morning at 46 Alexander Street in Rochester, New York. We sat on the ornate cast-iron steps that led to the first floor of the academy, waiting for the doors to open. Karl had been a student all his life and, knowing what to expect, was ready for another academic adventure. I sat there, torn between hope and fear and not knowing what to expect. When the doors were opened, I first had to locate the dean, Dr. Ramaker to explain what I had done and ask whether the school would be willing to take a chance with me. Ramaker was a soft-spoken gentle person of few words. He listened to my story, then told me he would have to consult the rest of the faculty. Some time later he told me that they had agreed to give me a chance. The first year I would be on trial. If I could keep up with the rest of the freshman class, I would be able to continue, but if this proved impossible I would have to return to Canada. As I look back on that time now, it seems utterly incredible that I should have had a chance of survival. Some of it proved nightmarish but fortunately I had no knowledge of what to expect. So I began, taking one day at a time, until I emerged a new person living in a new universe.

The two primary languages in which subjects were taught were English and German; the two secondary languages required were Latin and Greek. German was the language I spoke, the language I had inherited from my parents, who had inherited it from theirs; we had always spoken it in a foreign country and without the benefit of academic refinement. It did not take me long to realize that my German was totally inadequate. Not only did we use a shoddy grammar and poor sentence construction but also a very limited vocabulary. This was the language I had relied on to facilitate my survival in school. Consequently one of my first requirements became the learning of correct classic German. With English my situation was even worse. I had just learned enough English to manage a few of the essentials of life. And as I was to learn, the school made no concessions for unqualified students; indeed, a number of them had to leave during my student years.

The semester began with *A Tale of Two Cities*. I don't know what the size of Charles Dickens' vocabulary was, but it soon became obvious that it was a great deal larger than mine! So I acquired a German-English dictionary and began to memorize new words after looking up their meanings. By the time I got through *A Tale of Two Cities* I had written so many German meanings between the lines that it was difficult to read the text. The dictionary became my constant companion. At night I took it to bed with me and placed it under my pillow. Every time a new word rose to my consciousness I pulled out the dictionary to make sure I knew its correct meaning. Interestingly enough, I soon developed an appreciation for the beauty of Dickens' style. I began to copy sentences and sometimes whole paragraphs into my notebook and memorize them in the hope that they would become a part of my English. From Dickens we went to George Eliot's *Silas Marner* and ended the semester with *Hamlet*. The final requirement for the class was to write an essay on the mental condition of Hamlet. By that time I was beginning to question my own sanity.

Latin and Greek presented other difficulties. Before I came to the campus the professor of languages had had a mental breakdown. His doctor had made the mistake of advising him that he would be able to return to teaching that fall if he did not exert himself. What the doctor did not know was that I was arriving on the campus that fall. I would spend my nights memorizing prepositions, declensions and irregular verb forms. Totally exhausted, I would stagger into the class the next morning having had very little sleep. The professor might have had a bad night of it himself. Sometimes he would point his long bony finger at me and say, "Mr. Bonikowsky, I want you to conjugate such and such a verb." Sometimes my mind would go blank and I could not remember whether I was in the Greek, Latin or English class. I would mumble whatever came into my mind. Still being quite frail from his illness, the old gentleman would lose his composure and order me out of the classroom. The dear man never knew how many times he almost drove me to the edge of the abyss.

Then there were textbooks on logic, chemistry, botany, and algebra. I did not know what these titles meant; the words had never been part of my vocabulary. The dictionary offered some help. I quit reading the Bible and clung to the dictionary, hoping that God would understand my plight.

Botany opened for me the first door into the mysterious world of nature. I could hardly believe what I saw and heard through Professor Meyer. He was as much a poet as a scientist and, like Albert Schweitzer, loved every tiny insect and respected every blade of grass. The long Friday afternoon excursions into fields and woods to examine some of the miracles of creation soon counted among the happiest hours of the week.

Taking algebra without ever having seen the multiplication table presented enormous difficulties. How I used to gnash my teeth over some of the assignments. The real tragedy arose out of the fact that there was no time to assimilate any of the material before the next daily assignment. I would try to comprehend its mystery, memorize what I could, and move on to the next formula. Now and then this house of cards would collapse. Very little became a permanent and integral part of my knowledge, which should be the case in a normal educational process. And what am I to say about astronomy, with its incredible exploration of the story of creation, of the orderliness and harmony of the spheres, of its immensity and timelessness, and of its predictability! Like Spinoza, I sometimes wept over the grandeur of creation.

When I first began to read Heinrich Heine's poetry, I had not known that words could be arranged into such beautiful, rhythmic sounds. I memorized as much of it as time would allow. Logic introduced me to the Aristotelian syllogism and taught me that reasoning must be clear and consequential and that conclusions must be determined by their premises. All of this burrowed its way into my metaphysics, where we have so much wishful thinking without proper attention to premises. And then there was the poetry of Wordsworth, his nature mysticism and his beautiful affinity with his sister Dorothy.

It must be said to the credit of the school, that it not only provided for the stimulation of the mind but that it also took good care of our bodies. The refectory was supervised by a German housemother who knew how to prepare simple but substantial meals. We lived in the dormitory which was housed in the upper three stories of a large building. The gymnasium, dining room, and laundry were on the basement level; the chapel, library and classrooms were on the main level. The school provided our meals and shelter while all other expenses had to be met by the student. The money to cover these needs had to be earned in some honorable manner. Some of the members of the student body of about sixty had a fairly good time of it. They either had inherited jobs from graduating students or they knew their way around. The odd jobs I did during those years in Rochester could fill a book. I planted gardens, polished office furniture at night when the doctors were gone, stoked coal furnaces during the midnight hours, staggering through the snow when I should have been able to get a little sleep. I simonized cars, repaired plumbing and painted houses. Sometimes I accepted a repair job over the telephone and when I got to the place the repair had to do with something I had never seen before nor knew anything about. This is where my creative efforts in Siberia and the Ukraine sometimes came to my rescue.

The real financial problem came during the summer when school was out. This was the time of the depression when it was so difficult to find any kind of work. I was afraid to leave school for the summer in case I should not be able to find a job or not be able to earn enough to return in the fall. For a number of summers I was able to work out an arrangement with the school administrator to care for the building and its garden for the privilege of living in my room. Sometimes I had to live on a few bowls of cornflakes a day. On an affluent Sunday, after church I would stop at the White Tower hamburger stand next to the Eastman School of Music and order two ten-cent hamburgers. Other times I had to be satisfied with one.

Sometimes I tried to find work by going from house to house, ringing doorbells and asking for any odd job that I might do -- only to have the door slammed in my face as if I were a dog. This should have been understandable, for the bread-lines were long in those days in American cities and beggars were everywhere. There were always people asking for odd jobs instead of being degraded by having to beg. I reached a point one day, when the door of a beautiful home on East Avenue was slammed in my face and the words which accompanied it were so devastating, that I resolved never again to ring a doorbell asking for work, even if I had to starve. It seemed like a brutal attack on something within me; I could not take any more abuse and humiliation. One result of these degrading experiences was that later, when I was living in my own home and someone came to my door wanting to sell something or ask for help, I invited them in, offered them a cup of coffee, talked with them, and tried to see if we could help each other. I have carefully tried to avoid insulting the inherent dignity which belongs to every human being. No one knows how many scars life may already have inflicted on a person and how close he may be to despair.

With the arrival of my first beautiful Rochester spring, the first year of my life at the Academy came to a close. In some respects this had been the most cruel year of my life. The physical and mental exhaustion and the emotional strain often drove me to the edge of despair. Had I not learned very soon, like the members of Alcoholics Anonymous, to take one day at a time, I doubt whether I would have survived the first year. Life had reached such a precarious balance that I was afraid to look for my mail, lest there should be nothing in my box, which might be enough to tip the scales. To reduce this risk, I arranged with a classmate next door to deliver the mail to my desk if there was any. I asked the faculty not to tell me what my grades were. I knew that if they were below the accepted academic standard, I would soon hear about it; if they should be acceptable but not measure up to what I expected of myself, the effect might be so debilitating as to threaten my survival at the school. I never saw all of my grades until years later, when I had to present my academic credentials to the University of Heidelberg. I felt so good about them then that before sending them to Germany I made photostatic copies for future reference. At Rochester I only knew that they had been acceptable, since I had not been asked to leave.

At the end of the first year when final examination time arrived, I slept less and less and worked longer and longer hours, until my waking hours seemed to be shrouded in a haze as the time of my possible Armageddon approached. I still remember walking into my classroom on a Friday afternoon for my last examination. Beyond that I have no recollection of what happened. I apparently finished the examination, then left the school not knowing what I was doing. Hours later one of my classmates came upon me in front of the Art Gallery on East Avenue, where he found me sitting on the curbstone playing in the sand. He put his arms around me and led me back to the dorm. I must have burned up every ounce of mental energy until there was not enough left to keep my rational faculties functioning. In a few days I had recovered, and since this ordeal had not been followed by an ultimatum from the faculty, I had the right to assume that I had survived the first year of academic life and would be allowed to remain.

Now came summer and the search for work. When none was to be found, I decided I would spend the time reading the German classics. This was before the age of air conditioners when the coolest place I knew in Rochester was the school gymnasium. There I spent my free hours lying on a tumbling mat and reading the works of Goethe, Schiller, Klopfstock, Storm, Heine and many others. What I did not realize was that these classics were to fix the style of my German speaking and writing for the years to come. Even now, when I visit Germany, my friends tell me that I do not speak contemporary German, but rather the German of the classics.

As my English vocabulary grew, I could read and understand more difficult books. I would, meanwhile, become terribly upset if a book came into my hands which I could not understand. Erroneously, I assumed that if a human being had written the book, I, being a member of the human family, should be able to understand it. No matter how difficult the content, I refused to give up.

Then came the day when I discovered the city library. I had no idea that mankind had found time, in addition to its struggle for survival, to write that many books and to record for posterity its experiences, insights and wisdom. Yet here they were, neatly arranged on shelves in front of me. I stood in the doorway, removed my hat and stared at the treasures in front of me. Here were the results of the efforts of countless men and women, for which some had to suffer and even die, and they were available to me for the borrowing. How grateful, I felt, we ought to be for the accumulated wisdom of mankind, written down over the last five thousand years since the invention of written communication by the Egyptians.

Overwhelmed by the abundance of available material, and aware of my slow reading ability and my brief time on earth, I early developed the habit of selecting my reading material carefully. Whenever I read something that contributed little to the growth of my knowledge, I felt I was neglecting my mind. And since time could not be recalled this would be an irrevocable loss. It has since struck me how unfortunate it is that so many people acquire the difficult art of reading, only to waste it for a lifetime by neglect or by the use of unworthy material. No wonder that the old sage, George Bernard Shaw, who certainly had done his share of good reading, said satirically that he became famous because most people get a new idea once a month and some get one once a week; but he had the habit of trying to find a new idea every day. If the reading public would make profitable use of this remarkable skill, there would be no market for the kind of dribble perpetrated on the public by radio, television and the press.

Sometimes I heard students discussing which subjects they enjoyed and which they hated, trying to find subjects in which it was easier to get a good grade, or singling out a professor who was more lenient. This struck me as an unfortunate preparation for life. It also indicated to me how little they had come to enjoy the gaining of new knowledge for its own sake, as an end in itself; rather they would take the easiest way out. Of course, there were differences in degrees, but generally everything seemed important to me. Did not all human knowledge deal with the substance of the world in which we live, and did this not imply that the more we know about the universe, the more rich and fulfilling life will be? I, too, have found some subjects more difficult than others, and some of them were terribly difficult, but I have not found these uninteresting.

During the first year or two, I was very much aware of my intellectual inferiority and my social inadequacies, so that I did little to satisfy my social needs. On weekends I would usually write the required essays, read, or prepare for the next week's classes. When a classmate would try to convince me to go on a double date, the thought horrified me. My only social outlet was within the school, and on Sunday morning within the church, which I never neglected and always found enriching. There was the question of social etiquette, which gave me a great deal of concern. For answers to such questions I would always look to Emily Post. How well I came to know that heavy volume! Whenever I ran into some problem at an evening gathering, I would stop in the library on my way to my room to consult this authority. In time I came to know the lady so well that if anyone had a question in her area of competence, I could advise exactly where to find the answer. However, slowly my confidence in this area grew also, and I overcame some of the social handicaps and began to move more freely into the world beyond school.

In reading the literature of Goethe, I came across a little volume entitled *Die Unterhaltungen zwischen Goethe und Eckerman* (Conversations between Goethe and Eckerman). These two men used to come together frequently for good conversation; it was the content of these talks that impressed me. How could two individuals achieve such a depth on so many subjects? In my experience I had never encountered anything of this nature. If this was possible a century or more before on the European continent, why not today on the American continent? Even in my half-literate condition I realized one would need a rich background of general and specific information and the stimulation of other minds to facilitate this kind of mental growth. This possibility challenged me. But unable to wait until I had accumulated such erudition (indeed, the day might never come), I did the next best and possible thing. I selected a few other students for whom the universe was not a closed book, for whom learning was a constant adventure, and for whom life had an aura of mystery and challenge. We came together for creative conversation. Since our other obligations came first, we had to meet late at night, frequently after midnight. We chose to meet in the bathroom so that we would be sufficiently isolated and would not disturb the others. Even there we would sometimes become so excited that our raised voices would disturb the slumber of our neighbours.

I was so impressed with the results that I would rush back to my room after the event to write some of the results down in the hope of preserving them for posterity. Fortunately they have not survived and posterity may be the better for it. But I am sure that these nocturnal encounters contributed significantly to my mental growth. It is through such experiences that thinking is clarified, ideas are refined and learning becomes embedded in the mental structure. There is no doubt that we never achieved the level of Goethe and Eckerman. Yet the rewards were such that, wherever I have lived since then, I have tried to bring together stimulating friends for intellectual exchange. Together we have gone over pleasant and difficult ground. To them I owe some of the happiest hours of my life, as well as some of the lasting insights which have come to me.

In the desperate effort to educate myself, I would rank reading first and conversation second. To converse stimulatingly and creatively, one must first have something of substance to contribute and I have found good books perhaps the most valuable resource.

During the years in Rochester, I usually bought my clothing second-hand or, if new, as cheaply as possible. Hence I would usually gravitate toward Front Street where, in addition to the overstocked inventory on the inside, wares were also exhibited on the sidewalk. I would do my purchasing in true Russian fashion. I told the merchant what I needed; he, in turn, would show me what he had and quote me a price. I would offer half as much, argue with him, and leave the store, sometimes after I had been insulted. A day later I might come back and bargain some more. This would go on until I felt that he had gone as low as he could; then I would buy the article. Later I would wonder whether I might not have been able to reduce the cost even more. One suit still stands out in my memory. Made of a fine piece of brown woolen fabric, it had been used as a display in a show window. As a result, the side exposed to the sun had changed colour. In the dim light of the store, this did not seem too threatening, and the owner was willing to let me have it for a reasonable price. But it looked different when I got home and saw it in full daylight. I wore it for a long time but I had to be careful whenever I confronted someone at close range and the light was bright. I had to stand sideways so that he or she would not be impressed by the two-tone effect, which ran through the middle of the suit from top to bottom.

Among all the odd jobs I did, one stands out in particular. I did gardening for a well-to-do couple. I very seldom saw the husband as he was usually at work, but what I saw of him gave evidence of a good and stable personality. With the wife there was a difference. Not yet introduced to psychology in school I did not know how to label her but she was emotionally quite unbalanced. I became the victim of her ever-changing moods. For instance, I had to transplant young trees, shrubs, flowers and even hedges to one side of the yard one week, only to reverse the process when I returned the next week. As a result, the beautiful garden began to look like a crazy quilt. Once I had to paint the kitchen in the darkest blue, only to have to change it to a pastel shade later. Since I was getting forty cents an hour, I was determined to endure the whims of this lost soul. It was, after all, her property and I was trying to earn a living. Why should I allow myself to be upset because of this woman's moods? But then something happened that made me realize the limitations of my tolerance. I had transplanted a twenty-foot hedge, down to the last sprig, to one side of the drive, covered up the deep scar I had made, fertilized the soil and planted some flowers. When I was called back the next week to return the hedge to its original place, something snapped deep inside of me. I left the yard and never saw the woman again.

Since I was doing a great deal of violence to my body by not taking the time to exercise it properly, I was having all kinds of physical complications. Dean Ramaker, who by this time must have gained some confidence in me, did a loving thing. When he heard of my difficulties, he presented me with a YMCA membership card for my second Christmas in Rochester. I went with it to the only place I knew which had a sign that seemed to match the lettering on my card. Many times I had gone on Sunday morning to Salem Evangelical Church on Franklin Avenue, and walked past the sign. I reported there one night at the desk, explained to the lady in charge who I was, showed her my card and asked for admittance into its membership. She in turn tried to convince me that I had come to the wrong place. I went outside, looked at the illuminated sign above the entrance and looked at my card. I noticed a slight difference in regards to the "M", but that seemed purely incidental. I returned to the desk once more and persisted in my determination to make use of the institution, but the lady remained adamant. I eventually realized what a profound difference could be expressed by an inverted M.

Rochester is especially blessed by a number of beautiful parks. One of the finest is Highland Park with its rich variety of lilacs. I am told that it is the largest lilac park in the world, with the greatest variety of this particular flora. It is here where I spent some of the loneliest hours of my life. I discovered that the more beautiful the surroundings, the greater the burden of loneliness can be. Some-times the sense of loneliness almost crushed my soul. It is reminiscent of the British poet who, during one of the hours of his deepest loneliness, walked out into the night. He came to the upper edge of the cliffs of Dover and screamed into the waves and the darkness below: "Is there any one out there?" In my case, though, people were all around me. During the long blooming season, when the air was saturated with the intoxicating scent of the lilacs, and young life was making love all about me, I used to meander lonely on a Sunday night over the winding pathways surrounded by the luxury of Mother Nature, homesick and unknown. How often I resolved, during these hours of silent despair, that if I ever found the life's companion of my dreams, I would come back to these idyllic fields to compensate for my present pain.

Back at school, a subject that gave me an undue amount of difficulty was Logic. It required a degree of abstract reasoning for which my primitive childhood, lived in the midst of an uneducated people whose thinking usually dealt with concrete objects, had failed to prepare me. It was easy to grasp the meaning of the Aristotelion system, but I got lost in the labyrinthine ways that were supposed to illustrate his system. I was unable to reduce its substance to subjectivity. It continually eluded my grasp, remaining out there, instead of becoming a part of the comprehensive structure of my thinking.

The subject of philosophy was even more elusive. For hours I sat in Dean Ramaker's class and listened to lectures that seemed to begin nowhere, floated through outer space, and ended nowhere nor touched any part of the life I knew and lived. There were, of course, other students in my class who had had a normal education but who also did not have the slightest notion of what was going on in our class. The difference was that it did not seem to bother them, while I felt humiliated and insulted. As the weeks went by I knew that before long I would be driven up the wall and would not be able to continue in this class. Something had to give. Sometimes when the professor realized how completely he had lost touch with some of us, he would reach deep down into life and use an illustration which often had to do with the intelligence of his dog. This was something I could grasp but the moment of recognizable reality would soon vanish. And there seemed to persist the implication that my sagacity was somehow associated with the intelligence of canines.

The time came when I could not continue in this world of unreality; either I would get some understanding of what this mortal was talking about, or else I would get out of this class and not return until I was certain that I could benefit from the lectures. We had left Plato, Aristotle, Maimonides and other luminaries on the philosophical horizon far behind and had arrived at the door of Kant, the greatest of them all. It happened that the professor of German gave as the weekend assignment the writing of a short essay illustrating certain elements in the German language. The fact that the crisis in philosophy coincided with this assignment in rhetoric led me to a desperate decision. I would try to express the essence of Kant's Critique of Pure Reason within the limitations of the essay in German or would admit that I had been unable to rise to the challenge of human thought raised by philosophy. That seemed like a formidable task, but I was desperate and knew that something radical would have to be attempted. I went to the library and got a few volumes that dealt to one degree or another with the principles of Kant's critiques. Returning to my room after lunch on Friday, I locked myself in so that no one would be able to interrupt my struggle with the Lucifer of metaphysics. I read and re-read, and when I got so tired that I could not go on any longer, I slept awhile and then returned to my task. Saturday passed without eating, still at the same job. Then, on Sunday morning, the miracle happened. If I have ever experienced a "conversion" this must have been it. It is difficult to explain just what happened. I broke through the confining walls of the concrete and tangible and found myself in a new and vast world of ideological dimensions. The wall between the real and the ideal, the physical and the metaphysical, between the timebound and the timeless, had suddenly yielded. Now the two worlds could flow together, interchange and reinforce each other. This experience was one of the most important revolutions in the slow awakening of my mind.

Now I was able to see what Plato had been talking about, what logic was trying to express. Much of the other material that had escaped my comprehension began to have meaning. When I returned to class the following Monday everything had changed. The professor was still using the same words as in weeks gone by, but they now tingled with content and a new reality. I had entered the world of ideas and was soon to find myself very much at home in this new environment.

The subject of physiology introduced me to another unbelievably miraculous world: the intricate organism that is man. I did not feel like the two little boys who got hold of a textbook in physiology while their parents were gone. When they came to the pages which contained a cross section of the human body, they were shocked by what they saw. Said one to the other, "Do you think that this is really true?" Replied the other, "If it's in a book it has to be true." Concluded the first, "Let's close the book and tell no one about it." It was different with me. The bone structure, the organs, the tissues, the nerve fibres filled me with amazement. Starting with a one-celled structure, how could the evolutionary process, over the eons of time, have come up with such an incredible biological structure? I wanted to know as much as I could about this phenomenon called man. Often I went to the room of the medical intern, who was teaching the course for the privilege of living in the academy, for more information and more books. I was familiar with the statement of the ancient poet who had declared that "man was fearfully and wonderfully made." But this was far more than I expected. The fearful part of his nature I had come to know quite well through the violence surrounding my childhood. Now I was being introduced to the wonderful side of him. While I had difficulty memorizing all the new names that this branch of science required, I had no difficulty in retaining a picture of the interrelatedness of every individual part.

Later on this picture was enlarged through biology and psychology and became even more miraculous. However, as my knowledge increased, I became increasingly more sensitive and even morbid at the sight of any suffering, human or animal. Today I am incapable of witnessing any cruelty or pain inflicted upon a living organism. Now every evidence of pain makes me aware of the intricate relatedness of all the parts and the neural connections that see to it that the whole organism is informed of the violence done to it. Torture or the deliberate perpetration of suffering upon others is completely incomprehensible to me. It has become impossible for me to remain objective or impartial. My whole being enters into the pain of the other, who becomes an extension of my own existence. Both my ethics and theology have become profoundly modified by this response to pain. Human greatness and the quality of life, for me, are determined by the extent to which we participate in the alleviation of suffering and the enrichment of life for others.

Sunday always found me in church and, as the many denominational and sectarian varieties were a novelty to me, I took full advantage of my freedom. My highest record for one Sunday was five services with five different sectarian labels. I wanted to make the acquaintance of as many of them as I could in the hope of learning something from each about the nature of man. I not only visited the principal Protestant sects, but also the Rosicrucians, Theosophists, Ethical Culturists, Bahais, and others. This may very well have been the beginning of what later developed into my commitment to the ecumenical movement. The two most extreme forms that I encountered, claiming their place within Christianity, were the Holy Rollers and the Spiritualists. After a number of visits to the Spiritualists and participation in a few seances, I came to the conclusion that they were a fraudulent aberration that had nothing to do with Christianity. The Holy Rollers, too, impressed me as a travesty upon the name Christian. One of these services, which included anointing with oil, and lasted until far after midnight, was particularly revolting to me. Near the end of the service, all those who desired the Baptism of the Holy Spirit were asked to come forward and kneel around the chancel. As many people started down the aisle I decided to join them, to avoid being identified as an outsider. Before long a few dozen knelt around the chancel, with arms outstretched, screaming, shouting, moaning, whimpering, and some praying in a recognizable language, while the minister tiptoed among them with his bottle of holy oil. In time these human wretches became exhausted and collapsed, so that before the night was over, in some places they were lying on top of each other like the refugees I had seen on the railroad platforms in Russia. Upon returning to my room at the school that night, I wanted to carry the experiment to its conclusion. I knelt, stretched my arms out and moaned. To my surprise I too very soon collapsed from exhaustion. What a pity, I thought, for these misguided souls trying to find a richer life in these barren fields. My experience with those who came together to speak in tongues (glossolalia) was hardly more elevating, and I could appreciate why St. Paul preferred to listen to someone who could be understood rather than those who spoke in tongues.

Why is it, I often wondered during those early years of discovery, that religion had to be turned into such a distortion of life? Did it not employ the same human faculties that are used in all the other areas of decision making, learning and growth? From whom do the evangelists receive their instruction? What is the basis of their mutilation of the process by which lives can become noble? Certainly not Jesus who, after he had decided on his ministry, called on his friends Simon, Andrew, James and John and invited them to leave their nets, follow him and find a richer life. They evidently did, and isn't this the way by which most good things in life are achieved? Don't we have to make up our minds if we want to amount to something in any given field? After the initial step has been sincerely taken, the individual has to proceed by subjecting himself to the disciplines, the efforts, the concentration, and the devotion to reach his goal. That is how the disciples did it and that is the way that still strikes me as the most trustworthy. Yet much of what I saw in those meetings in Rochester had little to do with the Biblical model.

As the desire grew to become a minister or perhaps a professor or public speaker, I wanted to hear as many outstanding speakers as possible. Sometimes I was completely disarmed by some of the oratorical demonstrations to which I was exposed. Sometimes I felt hopelessly disqualified for this field as a possibility. But as my confidence grew I made even more of an effort to qualify. Upon returning to my room after hearing an impressive speaker I would practice the dynamics of the speaker in front of my mirror. Only much later did I realize that in order to become an effective speaker one must, first of all, have something to say and believe in it deeply, and then the dynamics and choreography come naturally.

After four years in the academy the typical student was expected to graduate and thus be given the privilege of entering the seminary department, which provided three years of graduate studies. The climax, the final examination, came during another beautiful Rochester spring. The nightmarishness of earlier periods of examination had diminished, but to my surprise, my examination paper in philosophy was not returned. I did not have the courage to call Dean Ramaker to discover its fate. Some anxious waiting followed. Then one evening the telephone rang and the Dean invited me over for dinner. I immediately assumed that something had gone wrong and that the Dean had decided to let me know what had happened under the most favourable circumstances. I accepted the invitation, of course.

What happened that evening was to serve as a model for encouragement in crises yet to come. When I arrived I noticed for the first time that the Dean's hair had turned snow white. He had had me for four years in some of his classes! We sat down in opposite corners of the dining room. I still remember every picture on the walls, even the pattern in the rug. In vain I tried to think of something to talk about, while to the Dean, silence came more naturally. I could hear Mrs. Ramaker in the kitchen and quietly prayed that the meal would soon be ready so we could eat, and I could find out what this was all about. After we had been seated and grace had been expressed, the Dean looked across the table with a grin on his face and reminded me of the letter he had written four years ago, begging me not to show up at the school. "What has happened during the past four years," he said, "I felt deserved a celebration. Out of that freshman class you are the only one graduating from the department of philosphy with a magna cum laude, which is the highest honour this school can give to one of its students." If I ever enjoyed a dinner it was this one. Conversation soon began to flow freely, and when the evening was over I received my examination paper. The significance of this experience, after years of unending toil, always under the shadow of possible failure, only I was in a position to fully appreciate.

In the seminary that next fall I continued to work as hard as ever, but studying came easier now. I was slowly building up a background of information and the academic vacuum of my childhood was slowly being filled with essential information upon which I could construct new knowledge. I took advantage now of more opportunities to enter into the social life of the school and community, although I never allowed it to dominate too much of my time. Some of my classmates still thought me a bit abnormal, especially one of them. On his way out on each date, he had to pass my door and never failed to stop long enough to try to persuade me to join him. If I told him that I had found another interesting book, he assured me that no one was ever going to pay me an extra dime because I had read another book. There was no point trying to persuade him that I was not reading in order to earn an extra dime.

Since our school was only a few blocks from the women's dormitory of the Eastman School of Music, I am indebted for many rich experiences to the close proximity of the two institutions. Let me just mention one of these experiences. Among my friends at Eastman was one who deeply cared for me. She was a true artist and also deeply devoted to her violin. She had little free time, but never would miss a concert by the symphony orchestra or a major recital. My personal exposure to music was still limited to the balalaika, accordian or trumpet, the instruments of Russian folk music. I had never heard an orchestra. As both of us had little extra time, our dates were largely limited to concert nights. I did not explain to her that I had never been exposed to classical music, and what I had to endure during those first few concerts! Then I merely tolerated the music in order to be able to stroll with her during the intermission through the beautifully decorated foyer, with its rich red carpets and illuminated portraits on the walls. This gave me a feeling of wealth and aristocracy. Never before had I moved among such surroundings. Then I would sit through another hour of symphony for the privilege of accompanying her home to the dormitory.

But then one night, something happened that changed all of this. It must have been a great performance, as so many of them were under the leadership of Howard Hanson. That evening there was not only the symphony but in addition a large chorus. During the evening something began to change and my heart was strangely warmed, like that of John Wesley at Aldersgate. The climax came during the last number which began with a section of the symphony. Then other sections were added and finally the entire symphony and chorus. Suddenly I lost awareness of my individual identity in one glorious moment of transfiguration. I, the orchestra and the audience merged into one vast life-transcending harmony. All of creation and I had become one harmonious reality. How long I remained in that mystical state I do not know. But when it was over and I returned to normal consciousness, I knew that something significant had happened to me that night, that I had touched a new dimension of reality and that another wall had been broken down. When I looked about me, the audience had left; only my friend stood there, with her hand on my shoulder, smiling. Since that night I have returned to concert after concert, both here and in other parts of the world, and no longer for the purpose of enjoying an intermission. In time I lost my Eastman friend, but what she had done for me could never be erased. I have become a devotee of the arts, especially music, but also of architecture, monuments, and paintings. Much of the joy of existence, the outward reaches of my soul, and the nurture of my mystical potential have found their inspiration in the arts. For me, religious experiences and experiences inspired by art are inseparable and are part of the same dimension of reality, and both have played their part in whatever degree of redemption I have experienced.

Theologians, whose business it is to facilitate man's reach for the stars, have given far too little attention in their theory of redemption to the influence of the arts and to the power of beauty in the transformation of life into something more noble and divine. Of all the civilizations that have come and gone, the Greeks were the ones most deeply aware of the role of art and beauty in the molding of the mind and soul of rising generations. None of the world religions, including Christianity, gives adequate attention to this fact, even though religion has been one of the greatest sources of inspiration for artistic activity -- the purpose of its creations from cathedral to madonna, from a Bach chorale to stained glass windows, has been primarily for the glorification of God and not just to bring joy to life and to ennoble man's aspirations. Such a concept is unacceptable because it undermines the notion that man, born in sin, is too much of a reprobate to be lifted by the arts. He can only be saved by the primitive notion of a cruel human sacrifice called atonement.

Years later I went through Cryle Memorial Hospital in Cleveland, Ohio, where some of the most shattered lives of the last war were being rehabilitated. In one department I was able to observe what music therapy was able to do for these broken lives. I saw how patients, who seemed to be possessed by legions of antagonistic spirits, would, under the impact of classical music, become calm and relaxed and sometimes even radiant again. Such has been the power of music across the centuries, ever since David was compelled to play his harp to calm the restless spirit of Saul, and the Aeolian harps were used to entice the men of ancient ships. What a pity it is that so much of our contemporary life can rise no higher than what Dr. Sorokin has called "syncopated, counterpointed vulgarity" which is bereft of spiritual quality and can only address itself to the physical self.

It must have been during my first year in the seminary that I wrote a paper which greatly disturbed the professor of the New Testament. I had for the first time come upon the closing conversation of Socrates before he took the hemlock, as it has been recorded by his disciple Plato. I was deeply moved as I read these noble, inspired and heroic words. This, to me, was the ultimate test of a great and noble life. Here a man was freely accepting death rather than compromising his convictions and doing it in the hope of saving his fellow citizens from mental decadence and the young from an unexamined existence. At the same time I had been greatly disturbed by what the theologians, beginning with St. Paul, had done with the life and death of Jesus. They had deprived him of the nobility of freedom of choice by declaring him to have been predestined to die in order to appease the wrath of an offended deity. The one death was noble; the other, in its theological content, degrading. The one was an understandable historical event; the other was torn out of its natural historical context and forced into a preconceived theological notion. Furthermore, I found it difficult to reconcile this juridicial and merciless conception of God with the parables Jesus told about the Prodigal Son and the good Samaritan and with the susbstance of the Sermon on the Mount. The death of Socrates was an inevitable culmination of the quality of his life; the death of Jesus was made to appear as a contradiction of the values he tried to impart. All of this disturbed me so greatly that I decided to write a paper, comparing the death of Socrates with the death of Jesus, discussing their similarities as well as their differences.

I had no thought of being sacriligious or iconoclastic. I handled this as I had reacted to other problems. Here were two similar historical events, both of them tragic, and both of them a terrible indictment of social behavior. Why was the one allowed to remain understandable and clear in its historical setting while the other was shrouded in a mantle of theological mystery? In later years I read about Dr. Albert Schweitzer who was struck, even as a child, by the story of the shepherds and the wise men. He asked his father, "If these events actually happened at the birth of Jesus, why was there no attempt by any of these people to return and see what became of the child in later years?" These and other unresolved problems set Schweitzer out on *The Quest for the Historical Jesus*. I too had a question -- why were all other historical events that had come to my attention understandable, but when it came to a historical or mythological event in the Bible why did we have to turn to outside authorities for an explanation?

But whatever I had written in my search for more light, my professor saw it differently. He saw it as an attack on something terribly sacred about which questions should not be raised. I was called into his office to give further account of what I had in mind. Fortunately it had no damaging effect on our relationship, nor did it dampen my desire to express myself in complete sincerity on matters that presented a problem to me, rather than playing it safe by accepting the theological notions of others.

I had more than my share of contact with the professors. Another encounter of a similar nature occurred in the classroom of Dr Kaiser. We had completed Kirn's *Kirchliche Dogmatik,* and a number of other German scholars, as well as Thomas Aquinas with his teleological, cosmological and ontological proofs of the existence of God. Yet all of these had left me "orphaned as before; his love eluded still." Dr. Kaiser was a personalist and would have enjoyed it if all of us could have been satisfied with the acceptance of the picture of God as a Father and a Person. Since personality seemed to be the highest achievement of evolution, and perhaps the highest manifestation of life known to man, this attempt to conceive of God as a person seemed quite understandable. This impressed me however, at that time, as a form of arrogance. Because little man with his unreliable five senses and puny faculties could not conceive of anything higher than personality was hardly sufficient reason why the conception of God should be cast into this form. Had not Kant warned us that we must not construct the world of metaphysics according to the images of physical reality? I was concerned about the examination that had to follow at the end of this course and went to the professor to explain to him where I stood at that period in my thinking about the nature of God. To my surprise I found him very sympathetic toward my position and he encouraged me to simply express where I stood at the time.

Mention should also be made of the role of Salem Evangelical Church in my development. Situated on Franklin Avenue, it was one of the large churches in the city. There I worshipped regularly and sang in the choir under the direction of Professor Genhard of the Eastman School. Equally important, it was here I was given my first opportunity to use English in teaching. It strikes me now that I had never thought of the possibility, at the beginning of my student years, of preparing myself for an English-speaking ministry. That seemed to have been beyond my ken. There were at that time many churches, in both the U.S. and Canada, where the German language was used for the worship services and English in the work with young people. This was the goal I had in mind. I owe it to the kindness and confidence of others that I slowly outgrew that limited objective. I was given more and more opportunity to express myself in English. It was, however, Salem Church that gave me my first opportunity to teach a class of boys in the senior department. How well I did at that time I have no way of knowing. If I could get in touch with Joe Chris, who became a chemist with Eastman Kodak, or Bob Vogel who became a leader among the Quakers, they could tell me what they thought about my efforts at that time. They are the only two names I can remember from that class. In time the superintendent asked me to lead the singing during the opening assembly of the large senior department, and later to give the opening address each Sunday morning. In every instance of a new opportunity the initiative came from others, not from myself. I lacked the self-confidence to seek such experiences. Every request that came to me, came as a surprise. All I needed to do was to respond as best I could.

During the last year in the academy or the first year in the seminary a most unusual event took place. I received an invitation to come to one of the wealthy homes in Rochester. I accepted the invitation without any knowledge of its purpose. When I arrived on a Sunday evening, I found a group of young people already present, seated comfortably in a luxurious living room. After some general conversation, the mother took me into the kitchen and told me that she had heard me speaking to the young people one night in the Episcopal church. The reason she had invited me for the evening was because of a tragedy that had taken place in the family. Her daughter had been a student at the Sorbonne in Paris when the news reached her of the death of her greatly cherished little poodle. Unable to continue her studies, she had been brought home so that the family could help her in overcoming her grief. I was asked if I believed in the immortality of the little dog and if I would be willing to discuss the subject with the group. I was taken completely by surprise. While my personal immortality was still somewhat intact at that time, I was unsure what I could say in defense of the soul of a little poodle. But it soon became clear to me that this was more than a subject for casual conversation. The mother was serious, while the daughter sat there waiting in silence. What I relate here, as I try to recall that evening, is what emerged as I attempted to say something helpful at this unusual meeting.

Since I had had no preparation for this unexpected event, I had to rely on recollections from some of my reading, as well as some of the evolutionary material we had discussed with Dr. Meyer years earlier. He had spoken of the stream of evolution -- from the amoeba and protozoa, the unicellular creatures, to the most complex. He had informed us that there were no clear lines of demarcation between the lower and higher forms of life, only a change in structure and complexity; all of life was of one substance. It seemed obvious to me that there was no point along this evolutionary chain where something spiritual, some separate entity or soul had entered the body and a biological organism suddenly became immortal. If there was immortality, it had to belong to all of life, and not just to one organism among many. Hence, if we could believe in immortality at all, there was no reason to assume that the little dog did not share in it. This was not really a conviction on my part, but a logical deduction, as I had already become quite skeptical on the subject. Yet this was exactly what was needed on the subject that Sunday night. The effect on the daughter was immediate. This is what she wanted to believe, and now she had some evidence for it. There followed a rich and stimulating discussion, with lively participation by the group. The daughter had remained silent, but after cake and coffee, as I was leaving, she expressed her gratitude. The mother assured me that the evening had been all she hoped for. She was sure that her daughter would soon be able to return to her studies.

During the last two years in the seminary I was sent out in the summer to the German churches of North and South Dakota, to preach and to assist with the daily vacation church schools. I usually had more than one church, which meant that I had to speak from one to three times each Sunday morning, afternoon and evening. This was no small task, especially when the congregations began to follow me from one church to the next and I could not use the same sermon twice. The churches were so packed that some of the children had to sit around the perimeter of the chancel, facing the congregation. They would place their hands behind them for support and I had to be on guard constantly to avoid stepping on their fingers.

Out of this experience came the realization that if I was to become ordained and enter the ministry, I would not be able to serve among these people, or perhaps even this denomination. I would have to look for another denomination as a field of service for the future. My mind and spirit were developing in a direction that constantly widened the gulf between these people and myself. Their Biblical literalism and theological fundamentalism made no allowance for change or growth and was a religiously suffocating environment for me. I had to couch my convictions in a terminology that had become foreign to me, but was the only one they could accept without being disturbed! I had come to look at fundamentalism and dogmatism as a revolt against reason. I found the atmosphere stifling. There was no desire here for growth, no interest in new insight, and no anticipation of any new light breaking through. It was a religion that only looked backwards. It was anchored in the past, and looked with suspicion on anything unfamiliar. I needed an atmosphere in which I was free to express what I knew and felt and to seek new insights. Aside from religion, the cultural environment was not much better. It was almost impossible to find anyone in these small rural communities with whom one could sit down and discuss something of a stimulating nature. I tried teachers and was surprised how little they had to say beyond the limitations of the subjects they were teaching. I tried ministers in a number of denominations and fared little better. However, the hospitality and kindness of these people knew no bounds. I had dinner engagements for every Sunday during these summer programs, in addition to invitations extended during the week. At first this presented a bit of a social problem to me -- what to talk about? But in time a satisfying procedure evolved. Since I had spent a few years on the farm in Canada I knew my way around in their environment. We would usually pay a visit to the barns to see how things were going, have a look at the corn or wheat, then eat dinner, and after dinner usually look at the family album and hear tales from the annals of family history. This would round out a good and satisfying evening.

But there came times when I found it difficult to continue with this limited diet. One day I heard that a classmate of mine was coming by train through Bismarck, North Dakota. I was so starved for intellectual companionship that I rented a car, drove over a hundred miles, and waited for my friend at the station. When he arrived, I took him to a park where we talked all afternoon and much of the night. The next morning I returned him to the station where he boarded another train. On my way home I felt like a man who had just enjoyed a luxurious bath. After this I knew that I could last a few weeks longer. But to think of this environment as a setting for my future life had, by this time, become quite impossible.

As I was not ready to have my formal education cease after graduating from the German Seminary, and I was not sure whether I could make it at a university, I decided to take a course at Rochester University during my last year at the seminary and Karl Korella joined me. Since I passed this course in anthropology in good form, I felt that I could make it at any university. I had also been attending lectures in many parts of the city during the years in Rochester. Some of the additional lectures I attended were given at Colgate Rochester Divinity School, especially under the church historian Dr. Moehlman. Another experience that endeared this institution to me was its president, Dr. Albert Beavin. Dr. Beavin would invite the German Seminary glee club, of which I was a member, to his beautiful home on their new campus at Highland Park once a year. Those visits introduced me to one of the finest homes and families it had ever been my privilege to know. Dr. and Mrs. Beavin were the perfect hosts. There was good conversation and recreation before dinner. After dinner we would gather around the grand piano and sing for them German choruses and folk songs until deep into the night.

I had also been the guest of Mrs. Rauschenbush a number of times, enjoying her gracious hospitality for an afternoon tea. Her sensitive spirit and what she told me about her husband, Walter Rauschenbush, helped me to appreciate that remarkable man years before I had an opportunity to read his books. He had died a few years before I came to America. He had been a lecturer at our seminary and at Colgate. I feel that all Christendom is indebted to the contributions he made to the field of a socially dynamic religion. A founder of the "social gospel movement," he believed a religion without social justice was an impossibility. He helped Christians to rediscover the ethical content of the Judeo-Christian heritage. I feel deeply, personally indebted to this pioneer of a responsible Christianity. Mrs. Rauschenbush presented me upon my graduation from Rochester Seminary a copy of her husband's *Prayer for The Social Awakening*, inscribed with her best wishes. For me it was the finest expression of a soul sensitive to every aspect of God's creation -- the world of nature, of man, and "all things that have breath". This little book of prayers became for me the most useful throughout my ministry. John Baillie's prayers came second.

The name Karl Barth was also coming to our attention during these years. Classmates of mine who were getting by on a minimum of effort were not disturbed by new prophets that appeared on the theological horizon, but I wanted to know what they had to say to our day, and especially what answers, if any, they might have to some of my unanswered questions. When his book, *Der Roemerbrief* (the Letter to the Romans) arrived at our library, I promptly took it to my room to see what light it had to shed on the "predicament of modern man". I did not get into it very far, when I came across a statement which I found difficult to believe. I took the book to one of my professors and had him read the paragraph but he could not quite see why I should be so upset about such a statement. To me, at that time, it represented a blow at the very heart of Christianity. Barth was saying that there was no necessary "continuity between the actions of God and the actions of man." If this was true, what was it that Christ had come to bring to mankind? Was it not to reveal the nature of God and to establish a "continuity" between the actions of God and those of man? Had he not been declared a "Mediator" between God and man? What then was the purpose of the Gospel? What was left for us to say in the pulpit? No doubt some of the danger I saw was the result of my own insecurity at the time, and the need I had for a coherent theological and ethical structure. In retrospect I can appreciate my indebtedness to those who threatened my position, but at the time I was still struggling for survival and felt myself threatened by some of these voices.

We had two literary organizations in the Academy, the Germania and the Philomathia, both of them adopted from a European tradition. I belonged to the Philomathia. Its primary purpose was to provide a forum for self-expression, for special lectures and for literary activity. Each year we put on at least one play for the school and its friends. This gave me an opportunity to perform in a number of German plays, two of them from the writings of Goethe. I had also had the opportunity to deliver a number of papers, one of them on the theory of genetics, which had suddenly exploded into my biological innocence, and the other on some of the findings of Margaret Mead. Once a professor from the University of Rochester lectured on hypnotism and I offered myself as a subject for a demonstration. This gave me the benefit of a subjective experience in this interesting field of mental phenomena.

In the spring of 1938 we received our diplomas from the Seminary. At this time the Seminary was not yet an accredited graduate school; but steps toward accreditation had already been started and were completed shortly after my graduation. Students who after graduation completed another two years of college were eligible for their B.D. I wanted to go further than another two years of college. Since my brother Erich had gone from Rochester to Sioux Falls College and liked the school, and since it offered me an assistantship in the German department, I decided to enter in the fall of 1938. The college was also situated in an area where there were opportunities to preach in German. Two churches invited me to become their minister, in the towns of Tripp and Parkston. Thus I left Rochester after seven years, and all that was associated with that incredible time, and moved to South Dakota.

Chapter 7

SIOUX FALLS COLLEGE

I began work at Sioux Falls in the Fall of 1938. Something happened that fall that gave me a comfortable place in this new student body. The college president's wife had instituted a tradition for the junior girls of the school that was to contribute to the refinement of their social graces. Its culmination each year was a formal banquet. This year they had decided to select six men from the student body to write an essay on *My Ideal Woman*. I was one of those chosen and so was the president of the student body, a very popular fellow. Some of the students were hoping that I would win in order to "take him down a notch or two." That was a contest I won and as a result was the only male guest at the banquet where I could elaborate on the content of my essay. After this event almost everyone knew me, and my standing in the student body was assured.

The two little churches were ninety miles from Sioux Falls, which made it necessary for me to have a car. I bought a vintage Ford which turned out to be a dreadful misfortune. To protect myself, I informed the churches that they would have to take full responsibility for the Ford, maintain it and keep it on the road so that I would not end up subsidising my ministry to them. As it turned out, this was a wise decision, for the church did little more than to provide me with an opportunity to preach and keep my car running. The car had cost me $300.00, which it had taken me years to save, some of it during the most destitute years of my life.

How fortunate it was that I escaped without a major accident during those two years. I had to preach at least twice every Sunday and then drive back for a Monday morning class. Usually I did not reach home until after midnight. Sometimes I was so sleepy and tired that I had to devise all sorts of means of keeping myself awake. I sang, recited poetry, or held on tightly to the bottom of my dashboard, which was so sharp that sometimes it cut my fingers, all in the hope of keeping my eyes open until I got home. A few times it happened that I did fall asleep for an undetermined duration, waking up just in time before I could complete an accident. In the winter there was the additional problem of keeping from freezing to death. The car had no heater, and the doors were so loose that on a snowy, stormy night, with the temperature below thirty, the snow would accumulate inside the car. It was not until a farmer introduced me to what he called "heavy duty underwear" that I found some relief from the cold.

During the summer I lived with the Klaus family in Parkston, who were gracious hosts, and who provided what transportation I needed with their elegant Buick.

It was during my first year at Sioux Falls that I discussed the possibility of my ordination with Dr. Johnson, a new and dear friend of mine, and minister of the First Baptist Church of the city. He had come to know me well enough to be very much concerned about my being accepted by an ordination council. Nevertheless, he called such a group of ministers together, and after some fatherly advice, I took my seat before the council. As the questioning continued I became more and more disturbed over the nature of this procedure. There was not a single question that required an ounce of reasoning or that would have given me an opportunity to express my beliefs about God, man, society or the ethical demands that Christ makes upon his followers. It was something of an inquisition to determine to what extent I deviated from the theological norms that had been substituted for a creative faith. When it came to the Virgin Birth I knew that I had no chance, surrounded by these gentlemen. All the work I had done with the school of Higher Text criticism and the J.E.D. and P. transmissions of the Old Testament did not cut any mustard here. Very likely these gentlemen had never heard of them. They were startled when I questioned the historicity of the Virgin Birth. There was nothing to discuss. The issue was simple: you either accepted or you were theologically disqualified. I accepted damnation as the lesser of the two alternatives. The council was dismissed and I had been disqualified.

Through algebra, chemistry, physics and astronomy I had come to believe in an orderly universe. For me theology and religion were not a world unto themselves, where the laws of nature did not apply. The empirically verified laws had to apply to all of creation. Nor was it possible for biology to escape the test of science. It made no sense to me that God should have taken millenia to refine the miracle of heterosexuality, in order to make possible the rich diversity of life, only to nullify the process when a rather important event was to take place. Furthermore, if the Virgin Birth was a historical fact, with all the uniqueness that this implies, why was it that Jesus never made reference to it or talked to his disciples about it? Why should we make something a test of orthodoxy which Jesus never required of his disciples? Or by what right can we make fun and laugh at all the other references to miraculous births in the lives of other world leaders but resort to the executioner's block when it comes to our own legendary and mythological traditions? Or what do those who are so fanatic on this issue do with the chaotic differences between the genealogy of Matthew and Luke, who each in his own way, by different routes, tries to prove, one through the male lineage that Jesus was the son of Abraham, and the other that he was the son of Adam, only to arrive at a Virgin Birth which nullifies all of their effort? Or why was Mark, the first Gospel writer, never informed about this matter? Or why did Paul insist that "he was descended from David according to the flesh"? I could hardly give my allegiance to something that contradicted all other known empirical data. But I had failed as far as these gentlemen, the custodians of our faith, were concerned and if I was to stay in the ministry I had to look for another council. I had to do what Albert Schweitzer did when he was turned down by the first examining board -- find another.

This time I called on a classmate of mine who knew me even better than Dr. Johnson and who warned me about a possible repetition of the previous council. But he promised to do what he could. This second council consisted of German Baptist ministers, which seemed even more foreboding, except for a few young ministers of my generation who had read at least a few contemporary volumes. This council too, if anything, took less time to get to the Virgin Birth. But for this session I had come prepared with a possible fundamentalist solution. When we arrived at the fatal point, I simply responded that I held to the Markian, Pauline and Johnine tradition. These gentlemen must have assumed that there is only one monolithic treatment of the issue in the New Testament. When they wanted to know what I meant by that, I did what Jesus had done with the questioning young lawyer. I simply said that you must know the Scriptures and thus must certainly know what Mark, John and Paul thought. A lively discussion ensued which soon became so heated that I was completely overlooked. The time ran out and I was asked to leave the room and the vote was taken. I was told that it had certainly not been unanimous, but that there was a slight majority in favour of my ordination. I had overcome the final hurdle between myself and the Christian institutions out there. After a fellowship dinner at the host church, the council proceeded with the ceremony of ordination. It has struck me as unfortunate that theological students have to be examined by an assembly of ministers instead of by members of the faculty under whom they have studied and under whose nurture they had arrived at their positions.

At school every bit of my time was taken up by a full curriculum, by my two churches, the German classes, the international relations club and the Glee Club. Each year, during the Easter vacation, the choir went on a five state concert tour, in two chartered buses, which provided a rich experience for all of us. Somehow I managed to crowd into my two years at Sioux Falls a dramatic love affair. We shall call her Margot, a soloist in the choir and a talented, brilliant, attractive and ambitious lady of Irish background, with auburn hair, and a tremendous zest for life. Unfortunately she was Catholic but was willing to change her faith for the sake of my religion and profession. But I knew her well and doubted whether she would be able to change her faith. To worship with her in a Catholic church gave evidence enough of how deeply she had been conditioned by her childhood training. We dated for two years as often as we could, while in the meantime I read as much Catholic history and dogma as I could crowd into my time, to see if there was any possibility of my accepting her religion. Yet the more I read the more unacceptable this kind of authoritarian church became to me, an authoritarianism that had led to so much cruelty and denial of creative freedom. In addition there was the incredible corruption of some of the popes which made a mockery of the compassionate Christ. When

I attempted to compare this to the effort of Jesus to rid Judaism of its legalism, authoritarianism and ritualistic sterility, the comparison left me no choice. The most maddening aspect of this experience was that religion, which should be the great reconciler of mankind, was the only barrier that stood between Margot and myself and that prevented two human beings, in love with each other, to merge their destinies. I could see why Bertrand Russell was led to say that this kind of religion has inflicted more wounds upon society during the ages of its existence than any healing that may have resulted from it. As I look back on this experience now, in retrospect I feel that there might have been a remote chance if Pope John, a man with a deep appreciation of the spirit of Christ, had come earlier. As it was, I realized that reconciliation between these two extremes was impossible. We arranged for one last rendezvous in Chicago, to which both of us had to come from long distances, to bring to a fitting conclusion a beautiful and promising friendship. My knowledge of the history of Catholicism I owe to this encounter with one of its beautiful children. Again there had been much gained from this experience which I have been able to put to good use. It must be added that during the years of my ministry I have had the best relationships with my Catholic neighbours. A number of times Catholic theological students have come to my support when I was caught up in the civil rights struggle. When I was lecturing for the United Nations a group of Catholic nuns came to my support. I have even been invited to give an address in one of the Catholic cathedrals.

One of the most unhappy associations I had on campus was with a group of pre-theological students, a number of whom were already serving churches. There were a few fine men among them with whom it was easy to establish a meaningful and enjoyable relationship, but the atmosphere of the group was stifling for me. We met once a week for a pre-breakfast devotional period during which time it was usually impossible for me to achieve any degree of spiritual communion. It was dominated by a type of religious piosity and academic unreality that set it apart from every other group on the campus. Much of the fault may have been myself, but in this situation I could only use myself as a criterion.

The students in charge of the little college paper called the "Stylus" had offered me a column to which I could contribute whatever inspired or agitated my mind. Once I wrote something under the title *The Gods Created in the Image of Men*. I had meant no harm and there seemed to be an inexhaustible supply of historical evidence for this thesis. All the gods I had ever heard of had all been created by men. The reason why there were no two alike among the thousands that had been worshipped was that the tastes and aspirations of the individuals who created them were different. In addition they were the expression of different cultures and different societies. If one includes the religions of mankind there are a thousand different objects, from tree roots to mountains, that have served their devotees as a concretisation of their imaginary deities. Apparently my article was such a threat to the status quo that some of the campus divines called on me and raised so much unpleasantness that I decided to use my column less frequently.

With one additional summer course I was able to graduate with my BA in the summer of 1939. Then the problem arose of what to do next. I had by this time become so well adjusted to life on the campus that I was afraid to graduate and enter the cold, indifferent and competitive world beyond its protective walls. I was afraid to face life alone, away from the library, student friends, classrooms, and a faculty that thought well of me. To face the chilly winds of an impersonal society and start a new and different struggle for survival seemed more than I was willing to risk at the time. On the campus I was understood, my ideas were respected and all of this in an atmosphere that was culturally stimulating. Further more, I was still unmarried. I did not want to enter the ministry without a companion who understood me; who would be able to encourage me and "comfort me"; and who would be willing to help me build the kind of a home I was able to conceive in my imagination after years of social deprivation. After becoming a preacher and a part of a congregation, the opportunities to find the right person would be greatly limited. Finally, I felt that my own inner growth, which had started so late, had not yet reached a sufficient degree of maturity. There were important questions still to be settled and much that still needed the stimulation and nurture of campus life.

But where could I go next? I had written to the state University of Nebraska and asked for a teaching fellowship. For a time this seemed a possibility, until the university informed me that the enrollment was smaller than anticipated and that there would not be enough students to require an assistantship in German. Without any financial support, my chances were rather limited. Every dime I had earned so far had to go into education, to help my parents and to come to the rescue of a friend. During the years in Rochester I had somehow managed to save some $800.00. Then I ran into a family with two little children who were destitute. The father, though, was convinced that if I would help, he would be able to open his own gas station and establish a little business; then his family would be able to make it. Because of my ability to enter so easily into the suffering of others, I loaned him $650.00. When I was searching for a university and needed this amount desperately, he would not even answer my letters.

I turned to a seminary in the east, which I shall not name, which was willing to offer me a scholarship for further graduate work. Most of the details had been worked out and I was getting ready for my next adventure, when I received a questionnaire in the mail from the school. It was to be filled out and signed by me. What I could not believe was that it contained 12 articles of faith to which I was to sign my name. I was to do violence to my intellect and commit my mind to a formula that was setting limits on my freedom to grow. The only vision that rose before me was that of Mephistopheles demanding Faust's signature in order to gain control over his destiny. That I could not do.

It was now within four weeks of the opening of the fall semester. Not knowing which way to turn I went to the office of the college president in order to share my plight with him. While we were talking my eyes ran along his bookshelves until I suddenly saw the title *Realistic Theology*! So much of the theology I had been reading, both Continental and American, seemed to lack a sense of realism. If the premises could be accepted, the systems were logically convincing; nevertheless, they seemed unrealistic as far as the actual experiences of life were concerned. Here was someone who had made an attempt at realism. I asked for permission to read the book and excused myself. This has been the only theological volume that I read without interruption. I had the strange feeling as I read that I was entering a room in which all the furniture looked familiar, as if I had been there before. This was a theology as I had hoped it could be written. This dealt with real life, with experiences that were familiar to me. God was not the end result of a carefully arranged syllogism but a part of the very process of life itself. His kingdom had a social structure. And Christ was firmly rooted in history; he could be known, understood and followed. Having finished the book, I wanted to see who had written it. The author was Dr. Walter Marshall Horton, who occupied a chair of theology at Oberlin Graduate School. That meant little to me as I had never heard of Horton or Oberlin, except for an article I had seen a few years before, announcing the one hundredth anniversary of Oberlin College. I remembered that Oberlin was mentioned as the first coeducational school in America and the first one to admit blacks. But who was Horton, was he still teaching at Oberlin and could there still be a possibility of matriculating this late?

Chapter 8

OBERLIN: REALISTIC THEOLOGY

Within four weeks I arrived on the Oberlin campus and at the beginning of a new chapter in my life. There was no creed to ascribe to here; only an invitation to search, to learn and to build out of the new findings one's life and philosophy. Academically speaking I had never felt freer and theologically happier in my life!

But I was anxious to meet Horton and as I could not locate him, I had to wait until the night of the faculty-student reception. I attached myself to an older student and every time an aristocratic-looking, dignified elderly gentleman came through the door, I asked whether perhaps it was Horton. He was late, and when he entered he would have been the last one I would have suspected as the author of that book. Medium height, very unassuming, with a coat that did not quite fit and pants which were not the best match for the colour of the coat — that was Horton. That is how I came to know him and that is how he remained during the three years I was privileged to study under him. I shall forever remain indebted to him for the contribution he made to my life and thought. One of the impressions which was so indicative of his spirit and which may well be one of the characteristics of greatness became evident whenever a student asked a question. No matter how presumptuous, ill-informed or simplistic the question may have been, Dr. Horton treated it with his usual deep regard. Sometimes the class would break out in hilarious laughter over a question by a freshman. Horton would wait until all had settled down and then answer the question with the greatest of care, using all the resources at his disposal and treating it as if it were the most important question the student could have asked.

Here I experienced one of the finest examples of liberal theology. It happened in a seminar with Dr. Horton, called "My Personal Creed." We were required first to read all the historical creeds, analyze them, evaluate the content, the mode of expression, their relevancy to life and then come to these seminars to discuss our findings. When the semester ended we were each required to write our personal creed on the basis of what we had discovered and on the basis of what had become an intrinsic part of ourselves. Under such conditions one could find a faith to live by. This was the kind of approach to which my soul responded with deepest satisfaction. This was not selling one's soul to the lure of a Mephistopheles; this gave one a chance to discover who one was, what others had found meaningful and to allow a personal synthesis to emerge out of the experience.

An event occurred during my first week in Oberlin that undermined what confidence I had been able to marshal for my life at this graduate school. On the first Saturday night, after most students had left the dormitory for the week end and everything had become strangely quiet, I heard a shout coming from down the hallway. When I stepped out of my room I noticed a Chinese student at the other end of the hall. I had already met him at dinner in the dining room and went down the hall to see what might have happened. As I approached him he took me by the shoulders and forced me down on my knees in front of him, demanding that I pray to him because he had just become God. At first I took it for a peculiar variety of Chinese humour. Only a few hours earlier he had been a perfectly rational person. But when he persisted in his demand, I soon realized that something had gone tragically wrong with his mind. I took him to his room and tried to talk to him but he became increasingly more violent and I realized that I had to find some help. Not knowing where to turn, I called Dr. Horton. The moment he entered the room the man became quiet and obedient, like the demonic man in the presence of Jesus. He had to be taken to the hospital and later was committed to a mental institution. If this is what could happen to an established student in this graduate school, I thought, how long would I last? It was perfectly still in the building now. I was perhaps the only one left. What did I have a right to expect? What would become of me?

My most pressing concern was my need for work. Fortunately the English Baptist church on the edge of the campus was without a minister at this time, and I was invited to speak there on my first Sunday. During the following week a committee called on me and invited me to become their minister. I asked for a little time in order to find out more about the church -- what its traditions and practices were. I discovered two practices under which I could not accept their invitation: they were a closed communion, allowing none but members of Baptist churches to join in the sacrament, and there was one proviso of membership that was exclusionary. I reported this to the committee. I feared that this would close for me a most convenient opportunity, but in due time I was informed that the church had held a meeting and agreed to my conditions.

There was one communion service which I still remember. It was following the attack on Pearl Harbor when feelings began to run high against Orientals. I removed all the furniture from the chancel and invited a Japanese, a Chinese and a lady from Ceylon to join me around the communion table as a demonstration of our unity in Christian fellowship which transcends all racial and national barriers.

I remained minister of this church during my years at Oberlin. The decision to become minister had consequences which could not possibly have been foreseen. In the first place this was my first English speaking pulpit, something I had not anticipated at the beginning of my student life. Since I was first of all a student and only secondly a minister, this arrangement provided an excellent opportunity for me to discover whether I could qualify for a life-long English speaking ministry or whether I would have to continue to depend on my own denomination, to which I of course felt greatly indebted for the opportunities it had given me in life. Secondly, the college students who worshipped with us provided a real challenge for me to prepare sermons that would present religion in the context of the issues of our times in such a way as to catch the imaginations of a rising generation. I also met with students in church classes where they were able to discuss what had been said in the pulpit or come to a Sunday afternoon tea for the same purpose. I am forever indebted to these young and challenging minds for what they did for me in the evolution of a realistic theology.

But above all, this church helped to fulfill one of the most cherished dreams of my life. One Sunday morning a group of students from the conservatory entered the church. One or two of them were so stunning that concentration on worship and on the sermon became difficult. The group had been going to a different church each Sunday, at the beginning of the semester, to select the one in which they would become associate members during their time at Oberlin. This day they had come to test the student minister occupying the pulpit at First Baptist. They returned the next Sunday and the Sundays after that. One of them told me a year later that she had made up her mind on that first Sunday, because she was convinced that that minister had real possibilities. In time they became members of the conservatory choir and continued to enrich our worship with their music. Two out of this group served the church as organists later. But more importantly one of them later became my wife.

As my future in the ministry was still a bit unsettled at this time and I was thinking of the teaching profession as a possibility, I decided to work for an M.A. in philosophy under the guidance of Dr. Horton. In addition to the formal studies, this campus provided a rich variety of other cultural opportunities especially in music, as well as lectures by scholars from many parts of the world. After preparing for a lecture on John Frederick Oberlin, the European scholar and religious pioneer, I was convinced that this school was a splendid credit to his memory.

One of the difficulties, which had been an obstacle before but which became even more aggravated at Oberlin, was my eyes. Because of the endless amount of reading I had to do, a number of times they failed me completely and I had to stop reading for a week or more. I used to cover one eye and read with the other and when that eye gave out, I reversed the process. Once my general health got so poor in addition to the failure of my eyes that I had to take a number of weeks off. I went to a ministerial family in northern Michigan for my convalescence, where I entertained myself royally by participating in some of the winter sports. As soon as I could manage it, however, I returned to the Oberlin grindstone.

Another thing I did not find as easy as I had expected was the task of finding a subject on which to write a Masters thesis. At first I explored the possibility of writing in the field of humanism as I had been particularly impressed by the writings of Jacques Maritain, the Roman Catholic philosopher. But in time this subject seemed to present an insufficient challenge to me. My aim was not merely to acquire another degree; I wanted to do a piece of work that would lift my mind to a new level and open up fresh vistas. My next attempt was in the field of organised labor and the church. After having done a semester's worth of work in this area, I became convinced that my knowledge of organised labor was too academic and that I would have to join a union in order to get first-hand information. The union I consulted informed me that I could join only if I worked in a factory. So I secured a job with the Colson Corporation in Elyria, Ohio. This experience provided me with my first opportunity to have a close look at the age of industrialism. I lost my interest in the field as a subject for a thesis, but I remained with Colson for a year. Thus, for a brief period, I had full-time employment, was serving a church, carrying on graduate studies, and, while on the bus between Oberlin and Elyria, was searching for other thesis material by reading Spengler's *Decline of the West*, Kant, Hegel, Dostoyevsky and others.

Dr. Horton suggested that I try my hand at Karl Barth since I read him in the original. He did not know anything about the blow Barth had dealt me a few years earlier! I decided to give Barth another try to see if anything had changed. By this time the great theologians did not frighten me any more; I was secure enough in my own philosophy. Following Horton's suggestion I wrote a paper on Barth for a seminar. But again I felt that there was not enough to be gained from such an effort. Consequently I dropped the matter and gave my attention to other possibilities. I should add, however, that while I was moving from subject to subject in search of a stimulating challenge, I also had to meet stern demands in other areas of the curriculum. There was the Old Testament under Dr. May, a well-known scholar in his field. He gave me the only *grade C* I ever received in my graduate studies anywhere, because I was not able to squeeze enough preaching material out of the minor prophets. I always felt that just because material by one chance or another found its way into the Bible was no reason for having to find a sermon or two in it. There was also the New Testament under Dr. Craig; philosophy under Dr. Hamilton; and additional work under Dr. Stideley.

It was again a book that solved my problem. In my reading of Dostoyevsky I became aware, for the first time, of the Russian philosopher, Berdyaev, who is not well known in the West. Turning to his book *The Nature and Destiny of Man,* I found something on almost every page which stimulated my attention. I could sense the spiritual affinity between these two representatives of that fascinating body of humanity called the Russians. Soon interesting mental constructions began to take shape in my mind. I presented this new possibility to Dr. Horton who immediately endorsed it. I was soon so deeply lost in my recent discovery that I ate, drank, and saw visions in my dreams of Dostoyevsky and Berdyaev.

I need to insert at this point a most tragic event. Erich, after graduating from Sioux Falls, had taken another degree at Berkeley Seminary in California. He had also married and had just received a scholarship from Yale to complete work on his doctorate. He had not been feeling well for more than a year, but his condition had not been properly diagnosed. Doctors had told him that he was suffering from ulcers and he had taken appropriate treatments. Yet he died of cancer at the age of 32 in 1941, six months after his wedding. He had been a top flight student in Russia as well as in America. He was a gifted writer and was going to write the history of the Bonikowsky family. In the last letter he wrote me from the hospital he informed me that the doctors had given him up, the nurses had given him up, and as far as he knew, God had given him up, but he was determined to live. Only if his heart should stop would he accept defeat. In that case would I accept the responsibility to tell the story of our lives?

I had been at the wedding in Minot, North Dakota, and had to leave at midnight before all the wedding gifts had been unwrapped. During his critical illness I had been in regular correspondence with Erich and his wife. After his death she continued to write me every week. When the letters became more and more incoherent, I secured permission from the Oberlin faculty to visit her and remain as long as seemed necessary. When I returned to Minot I found her sitting in the parsonage, staring into space, and the room in exactly the same condition as I had left it at midnight six months earlier -- half the wedding gifts were still unwrapped. They had left right after the wedding for a honeymoon, but instead Erich had ended up in a hospital. So nothing had been touched since the wedding. It took me a number of days to make contact with her. She simply sat there in silence. When we finally began to communicate and she began to improve, I felt it was safe to leave. I know little of Erich's theology. I have no knowledge of the degree to which he had departed from the theological and biblical atmosphere in which he and I grew up. But I did find a manuscript in his library that pleased me very much. It was entitled *The Continuing Acts of the Apostles.* In the introduction Erich explained that he and the class with which he had graduated from the seminary had agreed that at the end of each year they would exchange with each other the most meaningful experiences they had had during the year. It made me happy to know that his religious point of view was not a backward-looking one, shrouded in what had happened in the past. The same illuminations that had transformed human lives in ages past were continuing and contemporary religious experiences were as important, if not more so, than what we have inherited from the past. The acts of the Apostles were continuing.

But we must return to my newly discovered Russian thinkers. I had some difficulties with them at first, but slowly the strange phantasmagoria of their world began to fall into place. The subhuman monsters as well as the individuals touched by sainthood in the tales of Dostoyevsky became identifiable creatures. With fear and trembling I began the first chapter of my thesis. As I had no way of knowing what anyone else would think of my work, I waited anxiously for the return of Dr. Horton, who had been ill and had gone to Florida to recuperate. When I was told that he had arrived, I slipped the part I had written under the door of his office and waited with great trepidation. Some time later he called me into his office and returned the manuscript with the encouragement that he would be glad to meet with any committee that might be called to pass on this thesis. I returned to my Russians with new determination.

Summertime provided no vacation for many of us who were always on the edge of a financial abyss. Vacations were the times when we tried to supplement our meager income so that we could finance the next school term. One year I was accepted by the Elgin Mental Institution near Chicago, where I had hoped to gain further knowledge about mental illness. But when, just before leaving, I discovered that I was only to receive room and board and laundry, I had to refuse this promising opportunity. Instead, a classmate of mine, Ray Giffen, and I allowed ourselves to be persuaded by a representative of the Electrolux Vacuum Cleaner Company to join their band of salesmen and sell cleaners during the summer. We were assured that some men were making up to $300.00 a week! Since Ray had a little old Ford, we agreed to try our fortune in the non-theological field of rug cleaning. After a brief training course in one of the hotels of Lorain, Ohio, and after we had been convinced that Electrolux could outclean anything in the field, we were on our way. We were told that in case we ran into any difficulty we could report back to the hotel any Monday morning for a "breaking down period." Any obstruction we had encountered would be dealt with by one of the top-notch salesmen in the field. We sold nothing and returned for further instruction. Inspired by new insight and a little courage and hope we would sally forth for another try. But before long the whole business appeared to me as grossly unethical. Here were poor people doing what I would have done, refusing to buy because they did not want to go deeper into debt. Yet we were supposed to break down their resistance and sell them something without which they could do very well. To achieve this end we were to use every psychological trick in the book. I had had enough of it, but Ray was still hoping for success.

But what suddenly brought this adventure to a disillusioning climax happened one afternoon. While Ray and I were demonstrating one of the machines in a home, someone robbed us of some of the equipment left in the car. This, plus the fact that we had sold nothing during an entire month and complicated by my rising moral scruples, caused us to give up this effort. What was left of this summer and the following summer I spent with a team of contract painters who taught me how to cover the largest area with a four-inch brush in the shortest time possible. I have no way of knowing how many gallons of paint I spread over a great variety of surfaces during those two summers. But here too I was being taken advantage of. As I was the youngest member of the team with the least seniority, I had to do the least desirable places. On the churches I was designated to do the spires. Once, while I was on top of a fifty-foot ladder, the whole business started to move and I found myself on top of the ladder suspended in space fifty feet above the ground. What held me in suspension was a rope leading from the ladder to the steeple.

Behind all of this dramatic activity, another and far more gentle drama was taking place. One of those charming students who had entered our church that Sunday morning a year ago was the gracious and always smiling

Helen Lindquist of Lawrence, Kansas. She was the daughter of Dr. G. E. E. Lindquist, the general secretary to the Indians of North America. Both of her parents were graduates of Oberlin. She was one of the promising students of the conservatory who had already won a number of violin contests. She had become a member of the church choir as well as of the discussion group. There were a few dates but nothing serious. I had been forced to live the life of a hermit for too many years to be able to enter easily into a promising commitment. How much I envy the students of today, especially in graduate school, who so often can find a partner with a job, who will lend them support. During my time that was almost unknown so that one had to wait. Furthermore, it became more and more difficult for me to make up my mind as the years passed. But the meetings with Helen became more frequent and more convincing. There were concerts, social events, lectures, long walks, and even bicycle trips that took us as far as Lorain, fifteen miles away. During all of this time the bonds of friendship continued to grow.

In the summer of 1943 Helen graduated from the conservatory as I was writing the last few chapters of my thesis. By this time we had agreed to get married that fall. Since I was again without funds, I had to stop work on my thesis, get a job with a landscaping company, and work from ten to fourteen hours a day loading dirt onto a truck and unloading it with a shovel. Sometimes the blisters on my hands made sleep at night difficult, but the vision of things to come kept courage alive. I took time out for a brief visit to Lawrence to see about final plans. What a reunion that was!

Then the day came when I bought a round trip bus ticket to Lawrence and a one way ticket for the Mrs. Bonny-to-be. There was $120.00 left for a honeymoon and perhaps the first month's rent for a small apartment. Upon arriving in Kansas City, on my way to the wedding, I had to change buses. When I put my hand in my pocket I found the money gone! At first I was simply stunned, then I started yelling, and finally I ran to locate a policeman. But as full consciousness returned I realized how totally unreasonable it was to do anything about it. The station was packed with people. All I had left were my two bus tickets. Crestfallen, I arrived at my wedding, which was a lovely affair, culminating in a garden reception. Dr. Lindquist offered to provide funds for a honeymoon, but with my sense of European economics I could not begin married life on a subsidy.

The Avon Chesbros, who were members of my church and a pair of the dearest people, offered us their home for as long as we wanted to stay. We lived with them for four weeks and then moved into our own little apartment of two rooms. Helen got a job at the college while I returned to my writing. The Colson

Corporation had been well impressed with my engineering talent and now asked me to come back to install some newly-developed precision machines, study their operations and teach a few men how to operate them. These had been recent innovations of the War Department. This proved to be one of the most crowded periods of my life. I had taken unto myself a wife, was finishing my thesis, serving a church, taking a few seminars at the school, and holding down a full-time job at the factory. The latter took ten hours out of each day, except Saturday and Sunday. But my health was good and I knew how to organize my time. There were no wasted minutes in the day. When my thesis was done and I had my M.A. I continued with my other work and began to look for a larger field of service.

It was quite clear by now that I was no longer limited to the German Baptists; I could enter any English-speaking field. The question I had to settle now had to do with the choice of a denomination. I was quite sure that I would have difficulty with the Baptists and they with me. But when Dr. Morris, the Ohio state Baptist conference leader, heard of my intentions to leave the denomination, he sent his assistant to Oberlin to discuss the matter with me. He was convinced that he could find a church for me in which I could be perfectly happy. He was so convincing that I agreed to preach in at least two churches that were looking for a minister. This I did, but when I met with the boards after the services to discuss matters, I decided not to take any further steps in this direction. I had to find a spot where I could breathe freely, where I could speak as I felt led, where convictions did not have to be couched in pietistic language, and where people were interested in exploring the adventure of life. Since I believed, with the mystic Jacob Boehme, that a person is above all else a Christian, and only secondarily a member of any of the denominations, this decision presented no problems to me. What I had learned from Methodist church history was very appealing to me. They had a well-educated ministry, a reasonably liberal pulpit, and a good organization. Many of my classmates at Oberlin were Methodists with whom I had a very enjoyable camaraderie. So I wrote the Methodist bishop about my interest. He, in turn, must have written to Dr. Williams, the Methodist minister who had the large Methodist church on the campus, and with whom I sometimes exchanged pulpits, to get some additional information about me. Dr. Williams took me out for a long car ride and convinced me that I should have an even more liberal pulpit than the Methodists could provide. His further concern was that I might not enjoy being moved around by the district superintendent, without having much choice in the matter. And he may have been right; I simply accepted his judgment.

And again, for the third time, it was a book that provided the answer. I was reading a book on church history and had read as far as the Congregationalists, about whom I knew little. As I was reading along I was suddenly struck by a phrase that I had never before encountered in the annals of theological formulations. I had come to the statement of faith, written at the denominational conference in 1913 in Kansas City. What I read was "I promise to walk in the ways of the Lord, made known *or to be made known to us"* (italics are mine). What a far cry from the Nicene and the Apostolic Creeds, each with their totally antiquated and meaningless construction. Here was something living, something that had been confirmed in my brother's continuing acts of the Apostles. This discovery, for me, must have had the same effect as the discovery of Luther, which changed his life when in reading the letter to the Romans, he came upon the words "the just shall live by faith." What I had discovered was progressive revelation, which had been the history of my own life from the day I learned to read my first book. I continued to read what I could find about the Congregationalists -- the freedom from external interference; the insistence on social justice; their educated ministry; and their emphasis on the importance of education. One of its founders, John Robinson, insisted that God could use an educated mind more effectively than an ignorant one. All this impressed me. Theirs was a theology in which there was room for new revelation, their treatment of the Bible was as a book in which the will of God could be found, instead of being "the word of God." All this was a theology worthy of serious attention. I wrote Dr. F. Fagley, the contemporary church historian, told him what I had discovered, and asked for any additional material. I found the little book *Christian Nurture*, a typical Congregational product that could only have been written within the bosom of this tradition. My choice was made. I applied for membership in this new denomination.

Before my next move I need to say a closing word about Dr. Horton. His *Realistic Theology* was responsible for my decision to commit my life to Christian Ministry. He became much more than a teacher to me. Of all the professors under whom I had studied, no one has spoken to my mind and heart as warmly as Dr. Horton. He became a dear friend and intimate companion. Whenever I ran into a blind alley, time spent in conversation with him seemed to open up new vistas. I came to love this genuine humanitarian. Before I left Oberlin, he suggested that if I could ever afford it, I should spend some time at a German university, and he suggested a number of them to me. Should I need a letter of introduction he would be glad to write one for me. He was known in the universities he had suggested to me. After attending Heidelberg a few years later, I called on him for the last time in Oberlin. Mrs. Horton had died and he had remarried. He had also had a stroke and was greatly handicapped as a result of it. When we enjoyed a cup of coffee and some ice cream, his wife had to assist him. I told him how much he had meant to me, but his modesty did not allow him to make a response. He just looked at me and took my hand. It was the last time I saw him. We exchanged a few more letters before his death.

Thus I have tried to trace my mental and spiritual pilgrimage from illiterate beginnings to advanced education. My years and work at Oberlin, the required writing of many papers which were read and discussed in seminars, and especially my work in connection with my thesis, helped me to achieve an integrated philosophical system, which left few strands of thought dangling in thin air. My thesis, *"The Nature and Destiny of Man According to Dostoyevsky and Berdyaev,"* was particularly helpful in the shaping of my *Weltanschauung*. I appreciated Oberlin's readiness to allow each student to develop in his own way. The emphasis was on scholarship and on good work; with this as the given, each student was allowed to follow his own Socratic daimonion and to achieve his richest self-realization. This, for me, is one of the most significant contributions of true education and liberalism. Since no one is capable of knowing truly what another's capacities are or what he is capable of becoming, schools need to provide the material and stimulus for growth. Oberlin provided this opportunity in a remarkable way.

Chapter 9

CLEVELAND: PILGRIM CHURCH

I was now ready to walk out into the world in spite of its threats, its competition and its uncertainties. Old Pilgrim Church in Cleveland, Ohio invited me to become director of its institutional work, and I accepted. Dr. Milton Grant, its senior minister, cherished great plans for its future. With a theater, bowling alleys, gymnasium, a youth canteen with some six hundred members, and an enormous sanctuary, the whole complex occupied half a city block and there was plenty to do! This was one of the first so called "institutional churches" in America, providing a variety of community services. It was built by some of the wealthy families in Cleveland and was one of the city's important landmarks. My particular responsibilities were to administer the educational program, to write an editorial every Tuesday, to manage the canteen, preach a sermon now and then and to share in the parish ministries. The buildings had been much neglected and since I have an incurable drive for physical labour, I put in endless hours on the physical properties as well.

About this time I changed my last name from Bonikowsky to Bonny, my adaptation to American society. Few knew how to pronounce the name, and even fewer knew how to write it. I found that when I stayed anywhere for a few days, I was soon referred to as "Bonny." I simply endorsed the practice.

I also started proceedings immediately toward becoming an American citizen. Until this time I had lived in this country on a student visa and had to report to the immigration office annually to prove that I was still fulfilling the student requirements. In 1946 I became a citizen. A year before this important event, something of greater consequence happened. In 1945, a day before Christmas, our little Beatrice was born. I had been working at the church on a large Christmas pageant and when I came home late that night, the telephone rang and a pleasant voice informed me that I had just become a father. I was so exhausted from all the work that had to be done in preparation for Christmas that at first, the announcement over the telephone hardly registered. After I had hung up, the impact of what I had heard slowly sank in. When I arrived at the hospital they wheeled that little bundle of humanity out into the hallway so I could see it. I could hardly believe what I saw -- an infant, but this time my infant. Her long black hair was sticking out in all directions like porcupine quills. While standing there in astonishment in the presence of this most recent miracle of the universe, the only word that came to me was "Putzi." I don't think that I had ever used the word before. I had no idea where it came from, apparently from some strand of German literature, but it stuck. And ever since that time she has remained my little Putzi. I have only seen the word twice since then in some of the German literature, and what it means is something comical or droll. For that Christmas day we had our own babe in the manger. And the child grew and increased in stature with God and man, and today is one of the national Congregational leaders. She has brought nothing but joy into our life and continues to enrich the family circle. She now has two promising children of her own.

Working in this big institution, which was now situated in a vast industrial community, I found it difficult to make contact with the families whose children were coming to our Sunday school. These were people from many different lands, who spoke a variety of languages and some of whom were illiterate. The men could often talk about little else than the jobs they were doing at the plant. To gain their respect and interest, I suggested to the Board of Deacons that I get a job at Republic Steel where some five thousand of them were working. This struck the board as a rather unusual approach to the program of Christian education, but in time I convinced them of its merits and they gave me time off to pursue my peculiar approach. I got a job that allowed me to walk for half a mile each day through the length of the plant collecting dust and steel specimens for the laboratory. By the time I left, I had come to know every stage in the fascinating process of producing steel. This changed everything. Now, when I called at some of those homes, I could ask the father of the family where he was working and what he was doing and join him in a discussion of his particular field of work. Some of these families in time found their way into the life of the church.

Because of the endless demands which this position made upon my time and energy, I found it impossible to find time for reading and the cultivation and nurture of my soul, which were so essential to my life. My health began to suffer. These circumstances led me, in the summer of 1946, to visit for a number of weeks the international Quaker community known as Pendle Hill near Philadelphia. This was during the time when Dr. Howard Brinton was "patron saint" of this remarkable institution. The life we lived there with people from many different lands, the rich and stimulating fellowship, and the quality of Quaker discipline did much to restore my soul. Here I also met for the last time Dr. Rufus Jones, in my opinion the dean of American mysticism, who had so much impressed me many years earlier when he had lectured at Colgate Rochester and my vocabulary was so limited that I had difficulty following his mystical flights. He died shortly after this last encounter at Pendle Hill, after a long and productive life, which has left its benediction upon countless lives in America and England. Of equal importance is the rich legacy of books he left behind to continue his ministry.

Chapter 10

ANTHONY: GERMANY REVISITED

Having served my apprenticeship in my first Congregational church, I found it necessary, for reasons of health, to find a less demanding situation and accepted the invitation of a church in Anthony, Kansas. When I first looked the place up on the map, I was convinced that I was not so sick as to go to what looked like the edge of civilization. But the conference minister persisted, telling me that I would have little to promote, no repairs to make on the buildings and plenty of time to read. All they wanted was a good sermon on Sunday morning. We decided to try Kansas, packed little Beatrice and Erich, our first son who had just been born, into our old Plymouth and crossed half of the American continent. It is to this auspicious circumstance that I owe much of the future happiness of my life. One of the first things we did was to announce in the paper a potluck dinner every other Wednesday night, to discuss ideas and books with anyone in the community who was interested.   The people responded and filled the dining area. They came from different denominations and we even had a few Mormons. This stirred my academically-oriented blood, and I began to breathe again. The letter of invitation had been right: I had little to promote and much time to read.

But something else was about to happen that I certainly had not anticipated when I first looked at the map of Kansas. There were two bank presidents in my congregation. In the fall of 1948 one of them asked whether I would be willing to speak at the farmer-banker banquet. When it was over I had a telephone call inviting me to have breakfast with someone I did not know. I met him at the hotel the next morning, where he introduced himself as one of the reporters of the Wichita Eagle. He had been at the banquet the night before, had made notes on my speech and wanted to know a little more about me. Soon invitations arrived from various clubs in Wichita, and then from other parts of the state, and then from surrounding states. They arrived from clubs, from churches, from schools, from 4-H clubs, and later from universities. Before long I had come to enjoy a new art, the art of public speaking, which provided countless hours of stimulation and enrichment.

But there was another dream that would not leave me. As far as I can recall it may have had its inception during those hot summer days, lying on a tumbling mat in Rochester reading the German classics. I am not certain now just when it began. It may also have been influenced by the fact that we had been sent to

Siberia because we spoke German, yet the family had never seen Germany nor lived there. And so the decision ripened that someday before I died I would visit the people who spoke this language and the people who had produced that literature. How I longed to see the Rhine, the Alps and the classic ruins of castles that I had pictured so vividly in the books of poetry. When Dr. Horton reinforced the dream by suggesting that I would enjoy and benefit from visiting a German university, the die was cast. I did the only immediate thing open to me; I started saving whatever I could from our income for the eventual realization of this hope.

Helen Bonny was devoted to her music. There had not been much opportunity in Cleveland to cultivate her art. But in Anthony she was determined to enrich community life with it. She joined the Hutchinson (Kansas) Symphony which provided a stimulating outlet; taught violin in the local school; and contributed music whenever a social occasion provided an opportunity. I had not realized how much she was devoted to her art until I watched her one day going from door to door, trying to sell tickets for a symphony concert in a town that perhaps had not seen a local concert for many years. When she had sold enough tickets, she brought an orchestra to Anthony.

With Helen's encouragement, along with her willingness to care alone for our family, to take care of the church and also to teach, I decided to share my hope with the congregation. To my surprise, I struck an immediate response in my church. After a number of discussions it was agreed that I could go to Heidelberg in 1950 if I would provide a speaker for every other Sunday, and for the Sundays in between, write a report from Europe that would be read from the pulpit by one of the deacons, in lieu of a sermon. The church would continue to pay my salary during my absence. Heidelberg in due course accepted my transcripts so that nothing stood in the way. In April of 1950 I was aboard the Mauritania bound for France. One of the things that surprised me was that I had cherished this possibility for years, yet when the time finally arrived, none of the excitement I had anticipated materialized. It was not until I was aboard ship and a German band started playing one of the familiar German folk songs that my cheeks became wet and I experienced the emotional impact.

What I experienced, saw and felt during those months in Germany and at the university would be difficult to capture in a few paragraphs. Most of Germany's cities were still piles of rubble. What I had read during the war did not begin to describe what I saw. Millions were still pouring over the Eastern borders, trying to find shelter in these ruins. One of the first things I did at the university was to find a community of refugees and join them. There were some thirty of us for whom a few elderly ladies were doing the cooking in a big kettle. Usually the soup consisted of cabbage, some potatoes and sometimes a few strips of bacon. A meal cost about twenty cents. They all became my friends because I was willing to identify with them and share their common lot. At the university some of the students were still coming to class without breakfast. They were only able to endure a few lectures and then had to be taken home. They had come to the tail end of what they called *Hoovering*. I knew that there was no such German word, and discovered that it was applied to the help supplied by the Hoover relief fund. They used to get one solid meal a day for a number of years; all that was left now was each Wednesday afternoon we received a chocolate bar, a carton of raisins, a sandwich and a cup of cocoa. What touched me deeply was that whenever they received these rations there was a large box next to the window, reminding them of their colleagues in East Berlin who were worse off, and many of the students shared their rations with these people.

I did not pursue any particular course of study. I wanted to get as broad an impression of the university as I could, and consequently attended lectures in over half a dozen subjects, from psychiatry to anthropology and much in between. Dr. Horton had been in touch with Dr. Emanuel Schlink, a Lutheran theologian on the faculty, who became my adviser. He provided rare hours of conversation for me in his home. I took his seminar on ecumenism and contributed to some of the lectures and discussions. But before long I was deeply involved with the student groups that met at night in different places. These men were the product of the Hitler Jugend, with its perverted social, moral and political concepts. For them not only the physical world had been reduced to rubble, but their whole *Weltanschauung*, their core of values, had been smashed. It was a deeply moving thing to share in their struggle to find some core of values to which they could commit their lives. We sometimes talked clear through the night and at dawn had to make our way back to the university for a nine o'clock lecture. Sometimes, to facilitate our discussions, we had ersatz coffee that defied description. Occasionally, someone would even manage to share a few pieces of cake with the others. It was during these hours that I sometimes saw a face light up and a student would put his arms around me as we were leaving and assure me that he could believe in life again. I also knelt at the edge of the Rhine, dipped my finger into its cool waters, and as the droplets returned to the turbulent stream, I recalled some of the history that had swirled around its shores since the Roman legions floated into these northern regions. I walked on the ruins of the Heidelberg Castle, pulled off some sprigs of ivy and recited some of the poetry dedicated to these remains of a glorious past. One day, while sitting in class, I suddenly recalled from my course at Rochester University the Heidelbergensis skull, which had long slipped from my memory. I asked the profesor in anthropology about its possible relationship to the city. He led me to the window and pointed at a peak along the Neckar River where it had been found. Next Sunday I climbed the mountain and explored his ancient home. Whatever we may think about this remote ancestor of ours, there is no question about his appreciation of beauty, to have built his home in this garden of Eden. From it one can look down the Neckar River with its luxurious wooded shore lines and at a panorama of exquisite splendor.

But I again began to dream of other possibilities. I was approaching the end of the semester at Heidelberg with an accumulation of experiences and memories that exceeded anything I had expected. Why not get a motorcycle, leave the university and explore more of Europe? And that is what I did. First I spent some time at the Ecumenical Institute in Chateau de Bossey near Geneva, listening to the foremost ecumenist, Dr. Kraemer, and serving as the German interpreter for some of the group discussions in the beautiful garden. Here we had theologians from a number of nations, including a priest of the Greek Orthodox church of Russia, now living in Parisian exile. He invited me to his church in Paris where I worshipped and later spent a rich afternoon in his modest garden in the city. I also met a representative of the church of Holland, a gracious lady, who arranged a garden tea for me in Holland a week later, to which she had invited representatives of her church for an inspiring afternoon. And finally I also spent a few days at the UNESCO House in Paris to have a look at its international program. Here I met the remarkable Sir Cluth Mackenzie of whom I will have something to say later.

But before me lay all of Europe like an open book with its unbelievable scenic beauty in the south, its kaleidoscope of architectural beauty and variety, its cathedrals and museums, and its artistic creations in Gothic, Baroque, and Rococco. I was equipped with a sleeping bag, a tarpaulin, a few books, a few pieces of sausage, some kuchen, a toothbrush and a safety razor. This is how I set out to see the European world, including the Scandinavian countries and England. I lived on two dollars a day, which included petrol for my little motorcycle. I slept out of doors in the mountains of Switzerland, the valleys of Austria, the forests of Germany, the canals of Holland, the hedges of England and beside lakes in Sweden. This was a chapter of my life without parallel. To drive a motorcycle from a mountain peak in Switzerland in the direction of Vienna, facing the rising sun, is an experience transcending language.

After a swing through the Scandinavian countries, I stopped at Bremen to spend a few days with my uncle, Gustaf Zozmann, whom I had never met. He had left Poland as a young man in the hope of finding work in Germany. It did not take long to realize that we had a great deal in common and that there was much to share between us about ideas. From here I returned to Heidelberg for a final farewell with my friends, and especially with Dr. Schlink who had meant so much to me during the months at the university. I had a final dinner with his family and, as was the custom, retired to his library for a cup of coffee and a final review of my impressions of Europe. We also talked about his predictions of the direction he thought religion might take in Europe after the devastation. Finally, after another brief stop in Paris I was on my way home to Anthony.

I was pleased to see how well things had gone at the church under the leadership of Helen. We were expecting our third child, who was to be born in Lawrence, rather than in the small hospital in Anthony. A few days after my arrival Helen left for Lawrence to stay with her parents. I had long since become a committed internationalist, committed to the United Nations as well as to UNESCO. What caught my attention was the preamble to the constitution of UNESCO, which begins with these words: "Since wars begin in the minds of

Rev. Bonny and family in Topeka, Kansas in 1967. Top row, left to right, Erich, Oscar, and Francis. Bottom, left to right, Helen and Beatrice Bonny.

men, it is in the minds of men that the defenses of peace must be contructed." That struck me as going to the root of the matter in the hideous institution of war. Hence I devoted some of my time to the promotion of peace in the minds of men. In Kansas UNESCO had received a great deal of attention because of its promotion by Dr. Milton Eisenhauer, chancellor of Manhattan University.

Before leaving for Europe I had been booked as one of the speakers for the state UNESCO conferences, not realizing the situation I might find myself in upon my return. As it was, while Helen left for the hospital, I left for the conference in another city, which had already begun. Upon my arrival I found that the conference was being addressed by a journalist from Minnesota. He must have been an outspoken isolationist to judge by what I was hearing. When he was through and my turn came, I decided to discard my notes and address myself directly to some of the ideas that had just been expressed. When I was through the audience rose in applause. I immediately returned to Lawrence, and a day or so later was informed that I had been nominated president of UNESCO for the state of Kansas.

In a day or two Francis Albert Bonny let his voice be heard on the plains of Kansas. In the hope of producing at least one little saint in the family, we named him after St. Francis of Assisi and Dr. Albert Schweitzer of Africa. It took some time to make this clear to him and to let him know what our expectations were.

These had been enjoyable years in Anthony, among an appreciative people and with plenty of time to read and many opportunities for speech making. Then, one Sunday morning a carload of people arrived from Kansas City. After the worship service, they took the family out for dinner and told us why they had come. Their story was quite a bleak one. Their minister had been compelled to leave under pressure. This had created two factions in the church, those for and those against the minister. The church was in debt and the treasury was empty. "But," the spokesman for the group concluded, "If you would be willing to come and save the church, we will do what we can for you." That looked like a real challenge, and I was impressed by the sincerity of the group that had come to see us.

Chapter 11

KANSAS CITY: A BRUSH WITH DEATH

I went to Kansas City, had a look at the community and the church, and a few weeks later, in 1952, our family of five moved to the new parish, Rosedale Congregational Church. We did not even know what the salary would be. But if any church ever lived up to its promise to do what they could, this one did. When one of the deacons, in a board meeting, raised the question as to what I was going to do about the split in the church, I told him that I had no intention of doing anything about it. I told the board that I assumed that we were Christians which implied some degree of commitment to Christ, who had a great deal to say about forgiveness. There were more important things to do than to review the past. The question never rose again.

The people responded and the church was soon filled. The debt was paid off, a building fund was established for a new sanctuary and the old building was renovated for the time being until something more constructive could be done. We remained for ten years, and after we left I have been back a number of times to occupy the pulpit. Helen Bonny, the children and I felt so much at home among these "dear hearts and friendly people," that when the time came to leave, it was a painful decision to make. My public speaking, which added so much stimulation to my life, grew out of all bounds, until one of the church members insisted that she become my booking agent to keep things under control and also to make the organizations pay something for my services. There came a time when I even accepted engagements on Sunday mornings before my eleven o'clock service. What brought this to an abrupt end was a Sunday when, after I spoke at the large Community Christian Church, I suddenly realized that I had to run to get back in time for my own service. Not able to find the appropriate exit from the church, I opened an emergency door and fell into the parking lot. I had torn my suit and was bleeding badly. I had an arrangement in my church that a number of deacons would meet me before the service in a little room next to the chancel, where we would put our arms around each other's shoulders before I entered the sanctuary. This morning I entered through a side door and when the deacons saw my condition they were shocked. One of them got to the kitchen, came back with a wet towel and did what he could for me. There was nothing we could do about my torn suit. That morning I resolved never again to address another congregation on Sunday morning before entering my own pulpit.

Because of my insatiable need for discussion, I recruited a group of promising men who met once a month. They soon felt that this was not enough and that we should meet every Tuesday. When we decided to leave Kansas City, ten years later, the group had a final breakfast meeting, at which time they presented me with a book by Dr. Tornie, into which each one had written what "The Bonny Club" had contributed to their life. They certainly knew what their presence and contributions had done for the enrichment of my own life. I will mention another group which provided a similar opportunity for stimulation and growth. We called it the Medical Student Forum which met in our home on Sunday afternoons for six years. Since the church was not far from the Kansas University Medical Center, some of the medical students worshipped with us. Out of these visits, the forum developed. We tried to meet for a few hours on Sunday afternoons, but often they were so deep into it that they decided to bring sandwiches so that we could continue into the evening.

When Dr. Lindquist retired, he and his wife moved to Palm Beach, Florida. This provided us an opportunity to spend a few happy vacations there. The minister of the Palm Beach Congregrational Church and I planned our vacations at the same time, so that I could occupy his pulpit while he was away. This was not only sound economics, but also provided me stimulating contacts with his parishioners.

During one of these vacations in 1960, I started work on my autobiography. On the day we arrived I brought my typewriter to the mahagony paneled church office, and started typing. After typing seventy pages I had to leave for a speaking engagement at a Kiwanis Club hotel luncheon. I had not been feeling well, but assumed it would pass. But I became very ill on my return to the office, and had to be taken to the hospital. There my condition was diagnosed as hepatitis.

I was not quite sure what that meant but soon became impressed when the medical intern would put on a mask and white gloves before he approached my bed. This special consideration in my 16-bed ward indicated I was a special case. There was little that could be done for me. I soon completely lost my appetite and became weaker day by day.

Since in that large ward of critically ill patients someone was dying almost every night, it struck me one evening that I would never leave the hospital alive. I had with me a copy of St. Augustine's *Confessions* as well as the *Confessions* of Rousseau, books I had expected to help me in writing my life story. By this time I had been reduced to drinking only grape fruit juice, the one substance for which I had some taste left. I mention this here because it was a stage I passed through as I realized my days on this planet were numbered. At first I panicked, unable to believe or accept it.

But before long a great calm settled over me and a process of disassociation from the world began. One by one important connections were dealt with. First came the church, its people, then Helen, and our children. It was the children that gave me the greatest difficulty—the love and companionship we had shared. What would they become as they grew up? Over the hours that followed I began to work on three mental tapes, one for each child — my impressions of their personalities, what they might become, and a sketch of my moral philosophy for life. When these mental pictures were completed, we tried to locate a tape recorder to give them reality. But a recorder was never found, and I had to reconcile myself to the fact that these mental images would have to die with me.

As the days were slipping away I tried to read St. Augustine, but found him quite meaningless. When I told a visiting theological student this, he could not believe I had not found help and meaning in his chapter on God. I read the chapter after he left, but it "left me orphaned as before."

It was entirely different with Rousseau! His earthiness, warm identity with ordinary life, his utter sincerity made my blood tingle! I had to laugh and began to respond to life gain. When the doctor came to my bed the next morning I asked him why I could not return to my family since nothing was being done to improve my condition. He had no objection. Early the next morning, before anyone was awake, I woke up with the biggest appetite I had ever had for breakfast. When Helen came in I told her in minute detail what I wanted for breakfast. She stood there in disbelief, but I insisted.

After breakfast I realized I was going to live. Vital juices began to course through my veins, my mind lit up, and the world took on new color. But what I could not have anticipated was the shock that came with the realization that I would live. The calm, the peaceful surrender, the acceptance disappeared. I had to face life again — the obligations, responsibilities, and commitments. There was the church, new sermons to write, speeches to make, board meetings to attend, a family to care for. I was simply overwhelmed. But soon the pieces began to fall into place and the traditional mosaic became recognizable.

When news of my illness reached Kansas City, my church and others interceded for me in prayer meetings and tried to encourage me through their letters. What I told no one was that I refused to pray for myself. I wanted no preferential treatment, no special consideration. I had no intention of begging for mercy; my religion would not allow that. But my church did more, and sent me money for a plane trip home. But I refused to leave the family. When energy began to return, I was determined to drive our car back. Upon arrival home I had reached the end of my endurance, and collapsed on the living room floor.

It was not until a few years later that a doctor took the time to explain to me the role the liver plays in maintaining health, and how much was at stake. But by then it was too late. I had violated every rule of normal recovery. One of the great benefits of this experience has been the fact that, since I have gone through the process of preparing myself for the final departure, death holds no threat for me.

After ten years in the church I felt it was a long enough time, and that the church might benefit from new leadership and an influx of new ideas. I had two invitations -- one from a newly built church in Oklahoma City, consisting mostly of young business families, who wanted me to carry on the kind of work I had done in Kansas City. The other invitation came from Seaman Church, in Topeka, Kansas. I would have much preferred to go to Oklahoma, but Helen was completing another degree at Kansas State University, in the field of music therapy under Dr. Gasten, one of the foremost scholars in the field. He insisted that there was nothing at the University of Oklahoma that could be of much value to her. For six weeks the church in Oklahoma called me every Saturday night to see whether we had made a decision, patiently hoping that we would accept their invitation. But we finally went to Topeka so that Helen could finish her degree and continue her research at a well-equipped laboratory at the Veteran's Hospital in Topeka. She could also benefit from the work done at the Menninger Psychiatric Foundation. The ten years spent in Kansas City had offered me a fullness of life far beyond anything I had ever expected of the ministry. The farewell banquet was a moving experience. Our lives had become deeply intertwined and we had intimately shared the joys and sorrows of this Christian community.

Chapter 12

TOPEKA: A RARE FRIENDSHIP

My sons and I decided to travel to Topeka, some sixty miles west, on our bicycles. When the story came out in the paper, Bill Rinner of the Rinner Construction Company decided to come to church that first Sunday to meet the man who would come to Topeka on a bicycle. The friendship that grew out of that first encounter has no parallel in my life. He was morally an extremely sensitive person, opposed to every form of injustice and to any conditions that degraded or humiliated another human being. I was deeply involved in the struggle for social justice, open housing, fair employment and rehabilitation of prisoners. Bill stood by me no matter what I felt I had to do. He could not always respond in person when I needed him. Once when I called for his support, and he was unable to leave the construction site in which he was involved, he assured me that I no longer needed to ask for his consent. He knew me well enough by then, and assured me that I could count on his support in whatever I felt I had to do. And he never failed me. Even after I left the church, Bill and I remained inseparable until the day of his premature death. No other friendship in my life brought greater rewards.

Our old chapel in Topeka had become crowded and the church began to talk about building a new sanctuary. After the idea was articulated, there was no stopping the momentum. I was surprised how little of the burden fell on me. We had a strong men's group with individuals who knew the ins and outs of such an undertaking. In one year we had a beautiful new sanctuary which I came to love from the Sunday of its dedication. My only input was a sermon, before the final plans were made, on architecture as an expression of human aspiration. Whatever I said that morning found expression in the final plans, perhaps purely by accident.

We had been worshipping in our new sanctuary for less than a year when an unexpected letter arrived from Baltimore, Maryland. It had been written by the Clerk of Homewood Friends Meeting, a Quaker organization. They were looking for an executive secretary and invited me to come to Baltimore, spend a few days in the city and have a chance to meet with members of the organization. I liked what I saw: the people, the city, the scenery, the universities and colleges, and, of course, the possibility of working with Quakers. But since they already had the dossiers of two dozen other candidates, I did not think that there was any reason for becoming enthusiastic about this possibility. Yet a week or two later I had a telephone call informing me that Homewood Friends would like me to accept the position. I asked for a little time to think it over; I went to the city library and got out the few books they had on the Quakers. I could also rejuvenate my impressions of the time I spent at Pendle Hill many years before. And there was the memory of the lectures I had given at weekend institutes at a number of universities for the American Friends Service Committee, the social concerns arm of the Quaker ministries.

But there was another matter about which I felt deeply, and that was my connection with my own denomination. I felt profoundly indebted to the Congregationalists and the opportunities that church had provided for me. I had enjoyed years of absolute freedom in the Congregational pulpit. As was to be expected, people did not always agree with the position I had to take, and some of them may have been opposed to what I said or did, but I was never denied the freedom to follow my own conscience. The only limitation from which I suffered was the limitation of my own intellect. This was so much more than I expected that I did not want to separate myself from such a splendid tradition. Hence I informed the Baltimore organization that I would be happy to accept its invitation if I would be allowed a dual membership. They informed me that it was a bit irregular, but that they would consult the rest of the meeting. Not more than a week later I was informed that they would be willing to accept such an arrangement. As a result, in the fall of 1968, we moved to Baltimore. This proved especially propitious for Helen, who was then able to join the staff of the Maryland Psychiatric Research Center in Catonsville, which had just been built and was then in the process of assembling a staff.

Chapter 13

BALTIMORE: THE QUAKERS

Ever since my first introduction to Quaker thought I had held this small band of devout people in the highest regard. Here was a religion that took seriously the Social Gospel to which I had been introduced by Dr. Rauschenbusch. For them religion without service was unthinkable; they were two sides of the same coin. Here was a group of Christians who had never been lost in the sacramentarianism of the rest of Christendom. There was no struggle over the form of baptism, because Jesus had not practiced it nor could it contribute anything to the enrichment of life. There were no seven sacraments here, as is the case with the Catholics; instead they looked upon all of creation as an expression of the activity of God and consequently a sacrament. Instead of looking upon one isolated meal as a sacrament, they declared that every meal shared with a friend becomes a eucharist. The ultimate provision of direction for the life of an individual is not some past revelation, Scriptural or otherwise, but the spirit of God (the inner light) that dwells within every human soul. But of equal importance is their rejection of all the traditional fragmentations of life, whether denominational, racial, sexual, social or national. When I was speaking in behalf of the United Nations and needed a transcendent point of view, it always impressed me that anything written by a Quaker was always based on a universal ethic instead of some individual preference. So I had finally arrived, near the end of my professional life, in a position with a religious society that appeared to practice what, I believe, constitutes the essence of the ministry of Jesus. What a different world this could be if Christendom had not become a monopoly of the theologians who forced the kindly deeds and ministrations of the Man of Galilee into a thousand different creeds and dogmas and then set out to shape the tools with which to keep the masses in subjection. I had finally come home; my soul and intellect had found the cradle of their nativity.

There were some things that I missed. Since song and music had played such an important part in the enrichment of my life ever since I was a child, I missed the singing. Since I had developed an appreciation for the art expressed in theological architecture and appointments, they represented another impoverishment, although their absence was less important. Yet without their absence the little band of Puritans that started with George Fox three hundred years ago in England would never have become known as Quakers. If they had started to build churches instead of meeting houses, and had started singing, they would have become just another variety of Protestant denominations. So we must be willing to bear that small sacrifice. Their form of worship, the practice of group mysticism, is the most difficult one in Christendom, because it robs the individual of all external supports, and compels him to confront, in deep silence, himself, creation, mankind and God. It allows the soul, the inner light, to emerge and to modify and ennoble man's daily existence.

As silence is the dominant fact of worship, there were no more sermons to write, no programs to mimeograph. Some of the pastoral ministries continued. The sick were to be called on, those confined to their homes were to be visited, and the bereaved needed support and encouragement. But most of my time was spent with students from local universities. We were in the midst of the hideous war in Vietnam. Many students were opposed to it but did not know whether they could accept an uncompromising position of conscientious objection. Since Quakers are not in the business of making converts, but look upon their lives as an opportunity for service, my position was that of discussing with students the implications of a commitment to a CO position and then allowing them to arrive at their own decision. Some of them became committed to a life of non-violence; others realized that it required more than they were able to accept.

Furthermore, my position at Homewood brought me many invitations to represent Quakers at church meetings, synagogues, conferences, and a variety of public forums. University lectures provided another opportunity for service. Another fact I appreciated in my new position was that I no longer had to be concerned about raising church budgets. Here one of my responsibilities was to select areas of human need and present them to the meeting for consideration. If it was felt that we should provide assistance, the meeting would take appropriate action. Homewood, being a well-endowed society, has and continues to render an admirable ministry of love and compassion in many areas of human need.

The first time I visited our Meeting House, which is located across the street from Hopkins University, I was impressed by our beautiful and well-appointed library. It struck me as a suitable place in which to create a cultural center for our community. I saw it as a place for book reviews, for lectures, for musical ensembles and the like. I soon realized also that there were literally thousands of retired people living in the general area of our meeting. I began to call at the high-rise apartments to make contact and to find out what Homewood could do to provide a larger ministry to the community. When the job became more than I could handle, I invited the ministers in our area to assist me. But they soon lost interest because of other obligations to their parish constituencies. However the city was beginning to get involved in the problem of housing its senior citizens and to provide a variety of services to them. This meant that professional assistance soon became available. The federal government got into the act and things began to happen. The services we now have available for the elderly are so much more than could have been anticipated. As I was one of the first to express a concern, I am still held in the highest regard, have enjoyed a number of recognition dinners, and have received other honours far beyond any deserved merits.

My next concern was to convert our spacious and little-used dining room into a Day Care Center for working mothers in the area. Homewood Friends responded immediately and, since we had a number of teachers in our membership, they took things in hand and helped to develop it. Friends agreed that this was not to be another meeting ground for children of the rich. It was to be a school in which the foundation for a democratic society was to be laid. One third of the children were to come from the well-to-do, one third from people on public assistance, and one third from parents who could pay part of the support. And it was to be an interracial center. With the help of knowledgeable and devoted people, we created a center that met these requirements and has become a model for the city and even the state. Universities have been sending us students who are majoring in early childhood education, to do some of their internship at our center. In spite of the fact that I had promised at the beginning that the center was not to become a financial burden to Homewood Friends, they have since found it necessary to give assistance to some of the children to the extent of many thousands of dollars a year.

But by this time my retirement was approaching, and I had decided to take that step in my life seriously. At 11:00 AM, on March 22, 1975, I became sixty-five years of age. At that moment I closed the door to my office and stepped into the open, now one of the senior members of the community I had helped to organize. Not only did I close the door to my office, but I also withdrew from many of the agencies and organizations in which I had been involved. I wanted to become a completely free person without appointments to keep, obligations to meet or demands to fill. My son Francis, who at that time was first trumpet player with the Venezuelan State Symphony, wrote me an important letter. Knowing that my retirement was approaching, he warned me against my obsessive organization of time and my insistence on having everything organized, with every day having its specific schedule to fulfill. He knew me well. His simple suggestion was that I should do the things that give me the greatest amount of pleasure "and allow a new style of life to emerge." That took a year or two but I have achieved it remarkably well.

Since the population of the retired members of our society is growing out of all proportion to the rest, some very helpful books have been written on the subject. One of the greatest dangers of retirement appears to be boredom, which can result in depression, feelings of uselessness and many other emotional complications. These in turn can lead to a variety of organic malfunctions, to surgery and often to a premature death. The suggestions these good books make for a rich retirement are manifold. At the top of the list, however, is having a rich diversity of interests and a refusal to allow life to shrink into a private little world. Since this was in keeping with my life-style anyway, I had no difficulties.

All I had to do was to find new points of interest to replace those I was eliminating since closing the doors on my office.

One interest I did not need to replace was my life-time commitment to tennis, which has brought me endless hours of pleasure and which has contributed so much to the tone and health of my body. To come home, after every cell in my body had been exhausted on the tennis court, make a tall glass of iced tea, lie down on the floor and rejoice over the glory of human existence, are moments to remember. I am perhaps the first American who, after returning home from a quadruple bypass at Hopkins, was back on the tennis court within a few weeks. And this was after I had turned seventy-two! Yes, tennis has to continue as long as I can move.

The rewards I have received from public speaking continue, now primarily through the occasional opportunity to occupy pulpits in some of the city churches. And there is reading, a lifetime of it, to which I owe most of the ideas that have enriched my life. There is also music, and in Baltimore this includes above all else our splendid symphony orchestra. There is the TV to which I have finally caved in, especially the programs that make me laugh, which is so important in the coloration of life and can contribute so much to health and well-being. And there is my large carpentry shop in my basement.

Since throughout my professional life homes were always provided for our family, I had no property when I retired, with the exception of my car. What little I had been able to save would have paid for a modest home, and there would have been nothing left. Hence I decided to buy a run-down home that I could get very reasonably, restore it myself, and use my savings to speculate on the stock market in the hope of creating for myself a few comfortable sunset hours of life. Practically on the day I retired, a friend called to let me know that there was an abandoned row house, just three blocks from my office, which had been boarded up by the city and which could be had very reasonably. That is the house I bought. I restored one room first so that I could move in. Then I restored the first floor so that I could rent it to students, and finally, in one year, the entire house had been restored and furnished to provide a comfortable home. Since I did all the work myself, the cost was minimal.

It was different with the stock market. Here was a novelty about which I knew nothing and for which I had had no use during the frugality of a lifetime. There was considerable time wasted in poor utilization of its potential, and there was considerable loss because of ignorance. But as everything I had managed to save was at stake, I learned quickly. Today I am comfortably situated, can travel during the summer anywhere I want to go in the world, and can meet all of my modest demands of life. As I sit here behind this typewriter today, recalling the little boy in Siberia, and the illiterate man on the steps of the Rochester Academy, I cannot believe that all of this could have happened to one human being in one lifetime. One night I was sitting in a magnificent concert hall in one of the German cities. The walls were hung with impressive tapestries, depicting scenes from Greek mythology, while the orchestra gave a majestic performance. Suddenly tears started streaming down my face, and I could find no explanation for it. Only later, much later, did I realize what had taken place. I had realized what had become of my life. After the house was completed and there was extra time available, I accepted responsibility for a number of city properties, which enabled me to use all the skills and tricks I had acquired during the odd jobs in Rochester. But after a few years this became too destructive of my freedom, and I decided to get out. Ever since my arrival in Baltimore Dean John Peabody of the Episcopal Cathedral had been a dear friend. Many times over the years I had spoken from his pulpit and addressed church organizations. Upon my retirement he asked if I would be interested in a part-time position on the cathedral staff. As that would have meant scheduled time, I declined the invitation. But when the Cathedral School came to me a year later and asked whether I would be interested in maintaining the school equipment and building whatever new facilities the school needed, I accepted immediately. By now I had a fully equipped carpentry shop in the basement of my house, and I had always enjoyed working with my hands. I was glad to accept this new responsibility. For some seven years I enjoyed my relationship with the staff and children of the school, and my relationship to the cathedral staff. To my great surprise, when the Dean retired and they presented him with tokens of appreciation for his decades of service, he in turn presented a large brass plaque to the cathedral. On it were recorded the names of those he felt had enriched the ministry of the institution and I found my name among them!! But with the progression of the years, when activity has to be determined by the energy available, we have to be willing to surrender even those things that may have given us a lifetime of pleasure.

But to relate the full story, there is an event to which I come with great reluctance. To me one of the supreme tragedies of our civilization is that so many people, whose lives begin at the weddding altar with so much promise, charm, romance and idealism, find their feelings fading into mutual intolerance. As I got deeper and deeper into a life-fulfilling work, Helen was also pursuing the cultivation of her talents and achieving more and more in her field of music therapy. In time she published a book on her findings, entitled *Music and Your Mind*. She gave lectures throughout North America and in a number of other countries. She has given many clinics across the country and has received a number of academic degrees for her research, including a Ph.D. As one of the tenets of my philosophy has been to facilitate the deepest self-fulfilment in those with whom I am privileged to share life on this planet, I never interfered with Helen's work. I experienced great satisfaction in her success, in the recognition she received from her colleagues, and the stimulation it provided for her life. My only sadness came as a result of having to watch her physical health, which had never been too good, deteriorating under the pressures of her work. As the years passed it became increasingly difficult to perpetuate the idealism on which our marriage was based. There had been a number of critical illnesses. And when she returned from a hospital stay in 1974, she had decided that she was no longer able to live in our home and also pursue her work. This closed our twenty-seven years of married life. It took me some five years and many agonizing moments to get beyond this misfortune.

But I will forever be grateful for the life we shared and the mother she has been to our three splendid children. Coming home one night when she was cradling little Beatrice in her arms, I was so struck by the beauty and meaning of the scene, that she became my Madonna. Her understanding heart, her gentle spirit and her deep affection were the foundations of our family life. Much of what the children are today we owe to what Helen contributed to the family.

Our children showed a rare wisdom when the separation finally came. They felt that it was the best solution for the impasse life had reached between father and mother, and have remained completely committed to each parent. Even for me the time came when I was able to accept an invitation for a family reunion. It was held at my home with Jane presiding as the caring hostess. And there have been many other memorable visits since then. Our children are our greatest joy on earth. Beatrice is now a member of the national staff for the United Church of Christ, and loves her denomination as much as her father did. Erich, after having been a successful electronics engineer for a number of years, felt that he would be happier in an area of social service. He quit his job, went back to the university and secured the necessary academic credentials for his present work in counselling. And Francis, who must have inherited some of his musical ability from his mother, travelled the world with the Glenn Miller Band, served as first trumpet player for the Venezuelan State Symphony, and now plays his trumpet on Broadway. Further assurance of our biological immortality has been provided in six grandchildren -- two for each of our children. What a blessing they are, now that one can play with them and enjoy them without having to take responsibility for them.

Jane Karkalits and I met at a week-end retreat at Pendle Hill a year after my divorce. She too had just gone through the trauma of a similar experience. The Pendle Hill meeting was followed by correspondence, a few exchanges of visits between Baltimore and New Jersey, and a few trips to Europe during summer vacations. Then Jane accepted a position with Georgetown University in Washington, which greatly facilitated week-end exchanges between the two cities. In time friendship grew into a deeply supportive companionship and we decided to merge our individual destinies. We were married in 1980 at a meeting for worship at the Quaker meeting house in Plainfield, New Jersey, in an intimate setting, surrounded by many friends. A few years ago Jane also retired from her position as social worker with special responsibility for children with developmental disabilities. We are now in a position to pursue our many interests, both here and abroad, in addition to time spent with our grandchildren. Jane also enjoys a rich relationship with her children, Dagny and Richard, as well as three grandchildren.

Oscar Bonny and Jane Karkalits on the day of their marriage at a Quaker Meeting for Worship in the Friends Meeting House In Plainfield, New Jersey in the summer of 1980. They gave their vows to each other in the Meeting House in the manner of the Religious Society of Friends.

We have now come to the end of my active life. I have dealt with thousands of miles of geography over which the Bonikowsky family has had to travel, most of it against their will. I have referred to some of the inhuman and often irrational historic forces that have impinged on our lives. And I have shared the agony of a mind and soul in their struggle against insurmountable odds of ignorance and a religious distortion of life, of social and physical hardship, in search of light and freedom. But before we begin the second part of this volume, I must here express my indebtedness to Gretchen, that wonderful angel in Canada, who was responsible for setting me out on this life-long quest. It is reported that Abraham Lincoln is supposed to have said, "All that I am or ever hope to be, I owe to my angel mother." These words apply equally to Gretchen.

If that dear child had accepted my proposal, I might still be walking behind a plow in Canada, and the cultural, philosophical and physical universe which I now inhabit would have forever remained a closed door to me. It is she who inadvertently reached deep down into my being and, in the words of Exupery, said: "You were meant to be greatly human." Much of what my life has become and what I am today, I owe to her good judgment in refusing to marry me.

Chapter 14

ON MAKING SPEECHES

Since public speaking became so much a part of my life and provided some of the richest emotional and intellectual rewards, I want to relate some of its accidental beginnings and its ever-enlarging circles. Strange as it may seem now, I did not have in mind preparing myself for an English-speaking public life when I arrived at the doors of the German academy. At that time in American history there were many German clubs across the country who were determined to keep German culture and the German language alive. I was myself later engaged by one of these clubs to teach German to their children on weekends. But, more important, there were many churches both in the United States and Canada still using the German language for their services. If I were to become a minister, this was the field of service I had in mind. But my English vocabulary grew. I literally memorized thousands of words and their German meanings. In addition I copied into my scrap book sentences and paragraphs that I considered beautiful and committed them to memory, hoping that in time they would become a part of my vocabulary and style.

   Yet in the background something else was slowly emerging. Whenever I found myself in a social group, someone would invariably want to know about my background; who I was and where I had come from, and to the best of my ability I would try to answer these questions. Then came the time when I was invited to tell my story to youth organizations, church groups and others. Since this meant going over the same material again and again my facility improved and my confidence grew. I owe it to the kindness and confidence of others that I slowly outgrew my limited objective. I was given more and more opportunity to express myself in English. It was, however, Salem Church in Rochester that gave me my first opportunity to teach a class of boys in the Senior Department of its Sunday School. This happened long before I would have dared to look for an opportunity of this nature. When Mr. Than first approached me and invited me to become a member of his team of teachers, I was surprised indeed. On thinking it over, though, I came to the conclusion that Mr. Than, a successful business man and a person of culture and education, must recognize something in my potential that led him to this invitation. Hence he was really the one taking the major risk and not I. I accepted and before long was asked to give the opening address each Sunday to the large senior department, as well as lead the singing during the opening assembly. I found a lively pianist who was able to add drama to music, and the two of us with a few hundred young voices made the rafters ring!

Then came the first great opportunity. I was invited to give the opening address to a conference of young people in Buffalo, New York. Unfortunately the invitation had come to me two months before the conference. No one will know what agonies I endured during those weeks, how many outlines I made, tore up, made again, practiced in front of a large mirror and then discarded. You can imagine my surprise when I arrived for the opening night of the conference and, after travelling some eighty miles, found that my name was not even on the program. Instead I listened to someone else give the opening address! But when it was over I held no grudge against anyone. This might very well have been providential, both for me and for the conference. It could well have set back my aspiration for public speaking by years. What I was able to discover about the chain of events that had eliminated me from the program was that the original program chairman had suddenly died, and someone else had to move into his place who did not know what arrangements had already been made. Nevertheless, the ice had been broken, my name had entered the public domain and other opportunities soon followed.

When I was offered the pulpit of the First Baptist Church during my years at Oberlin, I had an excellent opportunity to experiment with my English. Here I was first of all a student, and only secondly a minister. This provided an ideal setting in which to find out how far I could get with my English. But Oberlin did much more than provide a testing ground for a possible English-speaking ministry. The challenge of having students in my congregation did a great deal to facilitate the development of a Realistic Theology. Often students challenged what I had said in the pulpit and I had to defend my position. I always had to keep them in mind when preparing my sermons. Here I became aware of the gulf that can exist between the way people experience their religion and the way theologians write about it. But Oberlin also convinced me that I was no longer limited to a German-speaking ministry, that I could now think of a much larger range of possibilities.

The next extension of my circle of public speaking came as a result of the farmer-banker's banquet in Anthony, to which I have already made reference. Upon my return from Europe, where I had also taken a look at the empty shell of the League of Nations in Geneva, a magnificent dream which America had left to die on the doorstep of Europe, I became very much concerned about the United Nations and the danger that it might face a similar demise if America should again go isolationist. Hence I offered my services free to the U. N. speaker's bureau in New York. This office kept us in touch with developments. The American Friends Service Committee, the social arm of the Quakers, had a similar concern, and had initiated a series of week-end conferences, dealing with international affairs, on university campuses. They invited me to join their team. Never before had I worked with a group of people like these Quakers. Their commitment to internationalism, to a planetary society and to peace and justice for all men, was an inspiration to me. Their eyes were fixed on a far horizon beyond nationalism, racism and other fragmentations that have made progress so difficult.

I have already mentioned Sir Cluth Mackenzie, whom I visited in the UNES-CO House in Paris. A giant of a man, blinded in World War I during a gas attack, he had set as the mission of his life to reduce the Braille dialects of the world to a single universal one, so that even poor nations would be able to provide reading material for their blind populations. In his large office the walls were hung with the Braille dialects of the world. While I watched him, he went from panel to panel, and explained to me the differences, and why there is so much difficulty in providing reading material for more than eighty million blind. I was so impressed by his story, that I resolved, upon my return, to do what I could to raise funds for his efforts. I told my story to farm organizations in Kansas, to PTA's, to 4-H clubs, to Future Farmers of America, and to others. Each contributed what they could. Upon moving to Kansas City, the children of my church used to go out on Halloween for "Tricks or Pennies." Other churches in the city read about it and took up the cause. Thousands of dollars were finally raised. Shortly before his death Sir Mackenzie wrote me to say that the job he had set out to do had been accomplished. The blind of the world now had a universal dialect.

One night, while speaking in one of the universities, there was in the audience someone who introduced himself as Dr. Benjamin Franklin. He invited me to join him for breakfast the next morning, when he told me that he was the president of the Associated Clubs of America, which was a network that covered much of the United States. He asked if I would be interested in joining his team of speakers. He was pleased with my interpretation of contemporary Russia. We were able to work out an agreement that for years took me to many states of the nation. I promised the church that I would always be in the pulpit on Sunday mornings, no matter where I was during the week. This promise was only broken once. These were all banquet meetings. I was to give a forty-five minute address and then remain available for questions as long as the chairman wanted the meeting to continue. Sometimes, after the formal part of the evening, a smaller group would take me to one of their homes or to a club in the city, to continue our discussion. After a night like this, when my whole being seemed fully engaged, I felt so rewarded that I could have sung the Hallelujah Chorus.

As my contract restricted me to the subject of Russia, I was greatly in need of reliable new information. Much of what I read in the American press was usually distorted to keep our paranoia alive. Since it was almost three decades since I had left Russia, I needed to bring my information up to date. The person to whom I am gratefully indebted is George Kennan, a great scholar, historian and a person of mature judgment. What a misfortune it is that we have a person of this stature in our midst, yet our political leaders refuse to use him in the making of international decisions. Here the myopic vision of the State Department and the Pentagon prevails. Kennan has called this the primitive intellectualism of the State Department. Robert Hutchins, former chancellor of the University of Chicago, has expressed it well when he said that so much of our attention is focused on Russia, constantly comparing to see whether we are ahead of them or getting behind, that if Russia should suddenly disappear, we would be lost. We would have nothing to compare ourselves with.

There was so much misinformation about Russia, that I decided to return to Russia for a first hand look at the society I had left many years ago. To avoid any risk and to take full advantage of such a visit, I waited until Stalin was dead. I returned in 1959. What I found astonished me. I was impressed with the new society -- its achievements in education, health, science, industry and even freedom. I travelled with a group of professional people, psychiatrists, teachers, architects, educators, doctors and others. In Russia we met with our professional equals, often in separate groups. At night the entire group received the information from each individual team. This resulted in a great deal more information. Since I felt very much at home in my native environment, I took a great deal of liberty to make as many contacts as possible, both with individuals and groups, from Leningrad to the Caspian Sea. I went again to Russia in 1966, and this time I tried to have as much contact as possible with the new Russian intelligentsia. There are many unfortunate limitations to Communism that will make it difficult or impossible for them to compete with a free and competitive West, unless it undergoes further significant changes. Until now their leadership has been incapable of initiating such changes. However the new leadership as represented by Mikhail Gorbachev is of a new quality and capable of bringing about these necessary changes. But of equal danger and limitation are the juvenile stereotypes with which we view the Russians. With our lack of historical knowledge and the maturity to make wise decisions, we continue to blunder out of one crisis into the next. Upon my return I had a great deal more information that I could use in my speeches.

Having shared in some of their suffering, I feel a deep kinship with the Russians, and knowing something of the forces that have influenced their history, they are less of an enigma to me than they are for many Westerners. They belong neither to the occident nor the orient; they are Eurasians, located in an area where the eastern and western blood freely intermingled, producing a unique society. Being tucked away in this vast hinterland, they remained completely untouched by many of the movements that helped to liberalize the West and made such rich contributions to our culture and life. They never knew the Reformation and other intellectual movements to which we owe so much. The Renaissance, which resulted in untold cultural benefits to the West, left Russia untouched. Fragmented by tribal traditions they were unable to defend themselves against centuries of foreign invasions, with their incredible destruction of property and life and the brutalization of society. They still speak over a hundred different dialects and their textbooks have to be written in more than fifty languages. A harsh climate and limitless horizons have shaped their temperament, their soul, their timelessness and their universalism. They are a people unique in their generosity, their hospitality, their bravery and their courage. A theme that runs like a leitmotif through their literature is that someday the world is going to find its reconcilitation in the vast, unprejudiced universalism of the Russian soul. These are people whose age-old struggle to be free has only led to centuries of suffering. Yet they have given birth to a religious mysticism, church music, architecture, and a literature that remains one of the great contributions to the culture of mankind. They are a people who constitute one of the great human potentials that has never been fully realized, but which one day will be free to enrich world civilization. Their government has been responsible for much of the suffering of my family, but their cultural achievements have also greatly enriched my life.

Public lectures were one thing, with a different audience every night, whose response I could predict with only a few exceptions. It was always, warm, challenging, and friendly. I would always begin with some humour, and after they had responded and were free to relax, I could count on their support for any intellectual flight. Sometimes they rose to their feet in spontaneous applause.

There are only three engagements that perhaps deserve special mention. One of them happened in Kansas City where I had been invited to address a breakfast club in the restaurant of the ornate railway station. Here were some thirty of the healthiest men I had ever looked upon. The head table was extravagantly decorated. Everyone had taken his seat, but the chair to my left remained empty. The men were getting restless as it was past the hour. I inquired about the delay and the chairman informed me that this was an occasion to honour the newly nominated beauty queen of Missouri, who was late. They finally had the breakfast served and suggested that I start my speech. I would stop when the queen arrived and allow introductions to take place, and then complete my presentation. After I was fifteen minutes into my speech her regal loveliness arrived, and every masculine eye in the room was focused upon her. Never had a public speaker faced a greater obstacle. After introductions I finished my speech, but everyone knew that it had become an exercise in futility.

Another event took place in Independence, Missouri, where I was to address a community Thanksgiving service in a hall not far from Harry Truman's home. I felt very much at ease, joined the packed auditorium for the singing of some of the great hymns, was introduced and then put my hand into the pocket where I normally carried my notes on small cards. The pocket was empty. My mind went blank for a moment. But as I regained my poise, I informed the audience about what had happened and asked them to sing another hymn, preferably a long one, while I made another outline. They responded heartily, and we were able to save the evening.

And finally, I was to speak at a banquet in the student union of Brigham Young University in Provo, Utah. It was an impressive occasion, a responsive audience, and the banquet an event to remember. At each plate was a cup of pink fruit juice that had been served with the meal. But my eyes were fixed on the strawberry shortcake, one of my favourites, with a good cup of coffee. I was waiting for the coffee. The people were starting their dessert and I turned to the chairman and asked about the coffee, only to be informed that there was no coffee in the building, nor tea or Pepsi. A doctor, who was my host, presented me with a book the next day entitled *The Best of Mormonism*. I read it and knew then that one must never expect a cup of coffee at a Mormon meeting. Furthermore, I was impressed by how many unhealthy habits these good people had identified long before there was much laboratory evidence to support their practice.

So much for the joy and stimulation that enriched my life as a result of the totally unanticipated opportunities of public speaking. It was different in the pulpit. Here I was surrounded by people whom I knew, who loved me and wished me well. Almost without exception I felt apprehensive and uneasy whenever I entered the pulpit. I found this a bit irrational and have only one possible explanation for it. It must have something to do with my childhood image of the deity; a judgmental being that ever overshadowed my life, especially when I was in the pulpit. Here I must have felt that I had to represent God, whereas with other audiences I only had to represent myself, my ideas and my convictions.

I did very little exegetical preaching, taking my clue from the Galilean. He certainly gave evidence that he had some familiarity with the religious literature of his people; however, only once, at the beginning of his ministry did he take his text from the Old Testament, reading from the prophet Isaiah. His sermons came from life. He dismissed much of the Old Testament, whose cruelty and legalism must have violated his sensitive spirit, by saying "it has been told you of old, but I say to you..." Here was a new sensitivity, a more refined morality, a deeper understanding of the complexity of the human personality, and a loftier conception of the Mosiac God. Jesus took his texts from the experiences of ordinary people: a farmer sowing a field; a grandmother trying to patch a pair of wornout pants; a mother baking bread for the family; the birds of the air; the flowers of the field; the bruised man along the roadside; a beggar starving at the gate of a rich man; and the tragic figure of a woman, caught by the custodians of a pitiless law. These are the things to which he gave his attention, so that people could see them against the background of a larger moral dimension of life. And they remembered them. I doubt whether much would have been remembered had he drifted into exegesis. A common accusation against him was that he did not give enough attention to the Hebrew scriptures.

We speak of and use past revelations, especially when it is of a Biblical nature, as if they had come down out of heaven in a galvanized pipe, especially if it is supposed to have happened 2000 years ago or more. The fact is that no revelation has ever gotten into history without having to pass through the protoplasm of a human being, all two hundred pounds of him! Whether the medium through which it has to pass is an illiterate, has a third grade education or lives in a primitive culture, all have their effect on whatever is transmitted. It must be obvious that the endless quotations in the Old Testament that are supposed to have come directly from Jehovah in the Hebrew language, must have had much of their origin in some other place than Heaven, as they contain so much cruelty and inhumanity. I am inclined to think that some of them must have had their origin with some primitive, nationalistic and ambitious adventurer.

How we can continue, at this stage of civilization and knowledge, to treat the Bible as something that dropped out of the sky, like the Golden Tablets of the Mormons, or the Koran dictated by the senior angel Gabriel, defies credulity. While in reality it had to come into existence like any other of the countless millions of books that have been written -- it had to be done by human beings, all sorts of human beings, with various degrees of insight, knowledge and ignorance. And if we are ever going to make sense out of it, and to come to know it for what it really is, we will have to learn to read it like any other book, without filtering it through an endless variety of concordances, commentaries and interpretations.

I saw the pulpit as an opportunity to try to lift the experiences of ordinary people, events and moral issues into a larger perspective. The ultimate business of religion, according to Schweitzer, is to develop more altruistic and compassionate human beings. All else is little more than interesting trappings. A great Chinese Christian scholar maintains that the aim of a religion must be to develop a supportive community in which no one will be abused. And I have no difficulty with that. Jesus may have had the same thing in mind. My preaching attempted to focus life on these ultimate moral values. I wanted to make people aware of their greater potential, of what human society was called to become. Someone has expressed it beautifully: *To help them see life in the light of eternity. I* always had my audience in mind. Sometimes, especially if there had been a tragic event in the parish, I would go into the pulpit early Sunday morning for the final review of my notes. I would imagine the audience in the pews, and try to make my sermon as relevant to the congregation as I could. Of course I used the Scriptures, but I never felt that every sermon had to be based on some text. If something was good and noble and could contribute to the enrichment of life and make it more sensitive, I did not feel that I had to find a text to support it. God did not cease to impart his wisdom with the closing of the Biblical canon. He was and still is doing what He has always done, communicating with His creation. The only grade *C* I ever got in one of the graduate schools was on an essay entitled *The Preaching Value of the Minor Prophets*. In addition, the professor had written across the front page, "Are these all the preaching values you can find in these prophets"? I am sure I could have found more, but I had seen too many ministers trying to squeeze blood out of turnips. Simply because a story or an event was selected by some committee to be included in the Bible was not enough reason that one should be able to extract a sermon from it. Now that I am retired and free to worship in many different churches, I am sometimes distressed by what is being done to the Scriptures in order to demonstrate the greatness of God and the glory of our religion. I am similarly distressed by the Biblical material used for liturgical purposes, which is anything but worthy of our emulation, sometimes reeking of Jewish nationalism. If the purpose of our religious experience is to foster the growth of kindness and love, we should be much more careful in the material we select for our worship service.

Once I had difficulty remaining through the entire service. The minister had chosen for his sermon an exegesis of the contest between the prophet Elijah and the 450 Baal prophets, which was to demonstrate the superiority of Jehovah. This bit of mythology is too well known to need detailed repetition. Suffice it to say that an altar was built and the Baal prophets called upon their deity to light the fire, but nothing happened. Then Elijah took over, and his God responded immediately, setting the wood on the altar aglow. This justified the Hebrew fanatic in his determination to murder every one of these innocent natives, whose crime it was that they remained loyal to the only religion they knew. Looking at the audience that day, they seemed to be pleased that our God had won another victory. Even the minister seemed to be pleased that he had made his point so convincingly. And this is what is called "the inspired Word of God." How much longer will it take for Christianity to produce a sufficiently enlightened leadership that will be able to recognize evil where it raises its ugly head, whether in the Bible or out of it? I need not take the time to speak of some of the enlightened American pulpiteers who have understood the mission of Jesus and provided inspiration and moral leadership for their congregations.

There have been some therapeutic side effects of my public speaking that deserve mention. When people first asked me to tell them something about my life, it often happened that I came to some traumatic incident that would not let me continue with my speech without taking time to manage my emotions. But as time went on, these incidents decreased. Therefore I had reason to believe that if I continued to tell my story, the healing process would in time overcome the wounds inflicted during my childhood. Not only did it reduce the pain, but it also diminished my nightmares. But then something happened which indicated that the healing process had not gone far enough.

Upon my return from my second trip to Russia in 1966, my family informed me that Dr. Zhivago by Boris Pasternak had been filmed and that I must try to see it. When it came to Kansas City, four of us from Topeka went to see it. What happened that night in the theatre is difficult to explain. It was as if my personality became unravelled and I disintegrated. I was overcome by a sense of panic, especially when it came to those dreadful winter scenes. I sat there and shivered. Since there was nothing I could do about it, I waited until the film was over and left the theatre as fast as I could. The only explanation I have for this experience is that there must have been too many scenes reminiscent of my childhood and that my body was unable to manage it. I had to ask someone else to drive me home while I sat there in silence. At home I went to my office and remained there until I regained my composure.

It so happened that a few days later Helen brought home as her dinner guest Dr. Stanislas Grof, a psychiatrist from Czechoslovakia, who had been giving lectures at the Menninger Foundation. I mentioned something of what had happened to me during the dinner conversation. After dinner Dr. Grof suggested that we go to my office, where I could tell him more about this experience and about my childhood. Before the evening was over he told me that there was now available a drug that had proven to be very helpful in similar cases. The drug was LSD, and if I was interested, he would be glad to give me a session. I went to the library the next day and read what I could find about the drug, most of which was of a threatening nature. Before Dr. Grof left town he gave me the first session. On a second lecture tour he administered the second session. I will not try to describe what happened, only to say something about the result.

Dr. Grof is, no doubt, the best known authority on LSD. He has worked with more than 2,600 patients in Czechoslovakia, Heidelberg, London and the U.S. He has now published a number of volumes on the subject, and is writing more. Some of his interpretations are quite technical and go into remote ramifications. I shall speak only of one of these theories which is particularly relevant to my situation. In essence the theory states that each of us carries deep within his subconscious the dreadful trauma of birth which the infant experiences as dying. If the early years of childhood are lived in a loving, pleasant, and caring environment, the original trauma is held in check and is unable to influence the emotional stability of the growing person. If, however, the child is born into a hostile environment, as was true in my case, the original trauma is nurtured and kept active by these additional threats. Sometimes this makes any kind of healthy living impossible, and can lead to mental and emotional illness. One answer to this threat is to create a condition that will make it possible for the individual to relive the death experience and through a process of rebirth, emerge to a healthier life.

Then, as fortune would have it, Dr. Grof was invited to become a member of the Catonsville research staff in Baltimore, at about the same time I was invited to come to Homewood Friends Meeting. This made it possible for us to continue the treatments; some of them were administered at the Psychiatric Center. Dr. Grof by now was quite optimistic that I was approaching the moment of rebirth. One day he invited me to his apartment for another session. Some twenty minutes after I had taken the drug, the miracle was in progress. I found myself in one of the great Russian cathedrals. As the music began and the cantor started to chant, filling the enormous interior with a great volume of music, the central dome of the cathedral exploded and the assembled peasants were sucked through the opening -- torsos, arms, legs and heads. Suddenly I felt myself lifted through the same opening into outer space. The joy, the harmony, the fusion with creation I felt was sheer ecstasy. I had lost my entity, become one with the universe, gone beyond life and death and entered a new realm. There was no more friction, no dissonance. I had returned to the cosmos from which I had emerged. In time I returned, carrying with me the memory of ultimate reconciliation. I had been "reborn." To this day the vision of a world restored and a wounded personality healed remain. To what extent this experience contributed to my present freedom, and feeling of joy and oneness with creation, I could not say. But I know that it has made its contribution to my pilgrimage from fear and dissonance to religious, philosophical and physical reconciliation.

One of the scenes that was a constant part of these sessions was of the Russian peasants in their wretched clothing, sometimes kneeling in fields of mud, arms outstretched toward the sky, begging for mercy. A number of times I asked Dr. Grof about these peasants. What had these miserable creatures, who had known little else but hunger, degradation and poverty, done to have to beg for mercy? Dr. Grof replied that he did not know but that sometime it may all become clear to me. Years later, during a summer when I spent some time in Oberammergau, I was reading in the morning and hiking in the afternoon. While reading a book one morning, totally unrelated to the peasants of Russia, the picture suddenly reappeared, and so did the answer. I saw it all very clearly -- these peasants begging for mercy were the people I had heard begging for mercy in my father's Wednesday prayer meetings, with arms outstretched toward heaven. When I had heard them as a child, I was afraid, and could not imagine what these good people could have done that required such demonstrations. Now I knew the answer: these Russians were the victims in the hands of an angry God, the God that haunted me during my childhood.

Chapter 15

THE HISTORICAL JESUS

It has been a long and sometimes lonely journey through a wilderness of distortions, historical accretions and misrepresentations to discover the gentle historic Galilean whose message was one of love and service: the man who had the capacity to identify with the humblest of creatures; the man who felt the heartbeat of humanity; and the man whose vision of the human potential transcended much of the cruelty, primitivism, and nationalism of the Old Testament. This man had come, not to fulfill some Messianic notion or traditional legalism, or to establish a new dogma, but to personify a new and creative way of life. Much of what he has been burdened with in Christian idolatry he never claimed for himself. Knowing himself to be human and aware of the limitations that human flesh is heir to, he rebuked those who persisted in calling him good, saying, "No one is good but God." He was driven by a desire to be helpful to others, to lift the burden of human suffering. He had little to do with the traditional authoritarianism in religion, but invited simple fishermen to join him in the discovery of a richer life. I respect and admire the great philosophers who have enriched my life and stimulated human progress with their insights, but I love Jesus for what he was and what he did.

But this admiration does not lift him beyond history or critical evaluation. He, as every other human being, was a child of his age and his culture, and consequently some of his teachings reflect the misconceptions and limitations of his time. Accepting the notion that the world was soon coming to an end, he promised to return in clouds of glory before his generation would have passed away. These were popular notions of his time. He said: "There are some among you here who shall not see death until the son of man returns." His advice "to take no thought for tomorrow" is only good advice if the time is short. Dr. Schweitzer has called this, in his significant book, *The Quest for the Historical Jesus,* an "interim ethic." And there have been countless misguided souls in each generation during these millenia, since the original disciples sold their property and waited for his return, who have proclaimed the gospel of the second coming, convinced that the time was now fulfilled and his return imminent. There have been those in every generation since then, including ours, who have kept these dire predictions alive. Some of our pulpits are pronouncing it, and our airwaves are filled with ominous predictions by swarms of evangelists that the last days and the second coming are now at hand. And the more limited their academic background and their grasp of human history, the more persistent their voices. It should be obvious to anyone that Jesus had no such conception of history. He spoke to his generation about things he expected to be fulfilled in their lifetime.

One is also struck by a number of contradictions and a variety of inconsistencies. He instructed his followers to practice forgiveness, even to their enemies only, for example, to condemn other undesirables to the torments of hell, a realm without pity or mercy, where there will be gnashing of teeth and everlasting roasting in a fiery pit. The American pulpeteer, Johnathan Edwards, who had a remarkable faculty for increasing the temperature of hell, had audiences swoon under his oratory. When father let loose on one of these texts, I used to cringe as a child, unable to imagine what any mortal could do to deserve such torture. How could any of this be reconciled with the gentleness and forgiving spirit of the Sermon on the Mount? Or consider the sin against the Holy Spirit, a crime that would never be forgiven. There is no indication what evil deed this is, but countless have been haunted to their graves by this threat, believing that they may have committed the unforgivable sin. As a child I did not escape this one either. What if I had done this nasty thing without realizing it? The result was that if I was ever caught away from home in a thunderstorm, I was sure that God might catch up with me; and I would run as fast as I could to get home and close to mother. I was sure that God would not dare to strike her. Cursing a fig tree or sending a bunch of swine to their premature graves seemed much less than we would have a right to expect from Jesus. And there was the whole matter of demonology, which permeated the atmosphere at the time of Jesus. As a child of his time, he, as well as Paul, accepted these evil spectres who were spreading disease and bringing untold harm to the lives of his people.

There was much to overcome and much more to leave behind before I could reach the historical Jesus, a person I could identify with and consider seriously. The ectoplasmic figure of my childhood, suspended between heaven and earth, was not one to entrust with my life. One of the significant experiences that changed this image for me was a course I took on the socio-ethical thought of mankind. Here we started with the earliest human writings of thousands of years ago -- the writings of China, Egypt, the Near East, the Hebrews, and the Greeks, clear up to the age of German rationalism. In each age we considered the quality of moral insight. Each important thinker was stripped of his embellishments and mythological trappings, and judged and evaluated like any other mortal, purely on the basis of his contribution to ethical insight and thought. Here I saw Jesus for the first time in the procession of other historical figures, having to demonstrate his moral contribution to the history of mankind. What mattered was his manhood as a moral being. Seeing him in this context, I was greatly impressed. It became clear to me why we only study Aristotle, Plato and Kant, but why millions over the centuries have made an attempt to follow Jesus' instructions. This is not to belittle the great leaders of other world religions, who have also made their contributions to the enrichment of moral sensitivity. It only means that what Jesus taught and how he lived awakened in me the deepest respect. Even a Napoleon, near the end of his life, had come to this conclusion: "Alexander, Caesar, Charlemagne, and I have founded great empires, but on what did these creations of our genius depend? Upon force! Jesus alone founded his empire on love, and to this very day millions would die for him. I think that I understand something of human nature, and I tell you that all these were men, and I am a man. None else is like him. Jesus Christ was more than a man."

Jesus gave substance to ethical monotheism as no one else in history. One of his unusual qualities is demonstrated in almost every encounter he had with his adversaries. Whenever they confronted him with an issue that required a decision, he possessed the faculty of placing his finger on what was universal in the situation instead of getting lost in irrelevant particulars. Every attempt on the part of his opponents to get him involved in fruitless theological discussions found him focusing in on the moral issues involved. When the lawyer asked him, "Teacher, what must I do to inherit eternal life?," no doubt anticipating a lecture on the metaphysics involved, Jesus got him to answer his own question. "Learn to love God and your neighbour and you will find the answer." Embarrassed, the lawyer saw an opening in another direction. "And who then is my neighbour?" he asked. Again, what he got was not an analysis of neighbourliness, but the immortal story of the Good Samaritan, which universalized the issue of social responsibility. When the Pharisees brought before him the woman caught in adultery, hoping to trick Jesus into a violation of Mosiac law, he looked at these advocates of a pitiless legalism and suggested that they had better take a good look at themselves first, and if anyone could be found among them without sin, he could cast the first stone. Humiliated, they took their leave, one by one. Loving even this fallen creature for whom society had no pity, Jesus did not condemn, but suggested that she try a new and more rewarding way of life. So it was with most of the issues posed to him. They were raised in the hope of involving Jesus in a fruitless discussion; instead they found themselves with a moral issue on their hands. This is one of the important characteristics that, for me, sets Jesus apart from other great religious leaders. Of equal importance is his insistence on breaking down the barriers between men and women, slave and free, Jew and Gentile, theology and ethics, ritual and conduct.

And here are a few more testimonies of how others have seen him. Rabbi Wise of New York had a picture of Jesus of Nazareth on one of the walls in his office. One day a friend asked him about the picture. Why would a Jew have Jesus on display? His answer was brief. "The greatest Jew in history." "But why," continued the friend, "a picture of the crucifixion?" His response — "The world's greatest tragedy."

Millions have said about him what George Washington Carver said about Simpson College. When asked what this school had done for him this remarkable child of slave parents replied: "It made me realize that I was a human being." Countless have recognized their deepest humanity in Jesus. Ibsen hailed him as the greatest rebel who ever lived. Will Durant spoke of him as "God's highest revelation". Professor Whitehead attested to his greatness by saying, "There is no more adequate test of a civilization than the degree to which the ideals of Jesus can be realized in that civilization." Walter Horton speaks of him as "The Eternal Contemporary" in a book of the same title. James Russell Lowell affirms his greatness saying, "Show me a place on this planet ten miles square where a man can live in decency, comfort and security, supporting and educating his children, a place where age is revered, infancy respected, womanhood honored, and human life held in due regard, and I will show you a place where the Gospel has gone before and laid the foundation." Lecomte du Nouy, looking into a future "undimmed by human tears," sees the coming of a day "when as a result of evolution, moral perfection latent in a small minority will blossom in the majority as will the universal comprehension and love radiated by Christ."

Thus runs the judgment of the ages in which his life and testimony have been put to the test, and during which countless other systems have been tried and failed. These testimonies are not the conclusions of a committee. These are the conclusions of millenia of human experience. To me the greatness of Jesus consists in the fact that he had a feeling for that which was eternally true and universal amid the chaotic mass of rubbish. It is this that makes him timeless and for humans eternal.

I know that most ministers and theologians make no or little distinction between Paul and Jesus, accepting their teachings with equal authenticity. The time came for me when I no longer could go to Paul for a better understanding of Jesus. Here was a man who never knew Jesus, and apparently made little effort to discover the moral demands upon which Jesus based his ministry. Steeped in the Pharisaic tradition of Judaism, and submerged in the sacrificial religion of the Old Testament, he set out to write a theology about Jesus. This forced the historical image of Jesus into the Old Testament atonement theory, which became the pattern of salvation for all of Christendom. Adam became the perfect man, which violates every scrap of anthropological history. This perfect man commits a sin; is driven out of his mythical garden; and offends a legalistic deity, who now, like a Shylock, demands his pound of flesh, before a reciprocal relationship can again be established. Jesus becomes the innocent victim who has to be sacrificed to appease an insulted deity. Henceforth mankind can again have access to God. This has become the pattern for humanity to this day, elaborated and embellished by countless theological voices across the centuries, beginning with Paul, reinforced by St. Augustine and transmitted from generation to generation. What does a theology of this nature have to do with the Sermon on the Mount, for me the most sensitive and noble statement of a refined religion, or with the story of the Prodigal?

The first followers of Jesus fortunately had no knowledge of this, and became disciples in the most natural way, by following their Master and attempting to learn from him. While Jesus insisted that a religion is useless unless it has moral consequences for human conduct, Paul came up with the theory that "the just shall live by faith," which later became the basis for the redemption of Luther. Paul may never have known that Jesus started his ministry with a text from Isaiah or have heard "let your light so shine among men that they may see your good works", and all the other references to deeds rather than faith. When John in prison wanted to know whether Jesus was the one that had been expected, Jesus did not send him an atonement theory. He let John know what was being done -- that the lame walk, lepers are healed, and the blind can see. When the disciples came to him, shortly before his death, to find out who would ultimately inherit the kingdom, Jesus repeated what had been the essence of his ministry: *I was hungry and you gave me to eat.* Far too much of the ethical substance of Christianity has been lost in the discussion of theological nebulae, instead of the challenge of purposeful living. The instruction is not by their theology you shall know them, but by their fruits ye shall know them. Paul's instructions in regards to slaves and women are an equal misrepresentation of the message of Jesus, who identified with them and demanded that they be treated as equals.

But the picture is not all negative. All I am saying is that I cannot put the two spokesmen for Christianity on the same footing. We must admit that it was Paul who saved the fledgling church from an early extinction by making it available to the non-Jewish world. It was his vision of Christ for humanity that liberated the church from being nothing more than a sect within Judaism. Had it not been liberated from its Jewish restrictions, especially dietary laws and circumcision, it would likely have disappeared within a century or two. By adapting it to the gentile world, it became available to all people. We are also indebted to Paul for whatever information we have about the original Christian community. And there are indeed beautiful examples of a mystical sensitivity and spiritual insight that have endeared Paul to many.

And finally a word about our rampant sectarianism. It was incomprehensible to me, when I arrived here, how we could have created over two hundred different religious groupings in America. How could these fragmentations have had their origin in the ministry of Jesus? How could these groups justify their existence? As a child I had become aware of three divisions: the Russian Orthodox, the Lutherans and the Baptists. In time I found out that there has perhaps not been a single split that had anything to do with what Jesus expected of his disciples. They all had their origin in some textual argument, and not over feeding the hungry, caring for the sick, or clothing the naked. You can't split over that; you need the Scriptures and theology to do that. I saw sectarianism as a blot on Christianity, and began to discuss mergers while still in the German Seminary. At that time I thought that it would be a good thing for the German Baptists of North America to unite with the American Baptists (English). I urged some of my classmates to join me, but they liked conditions as they were at that time, and I finally had to give up. When the ecumenical movement came along, years later, I became a part of it. One of my rewarding experiences was attending the Ecumenical Institute, near Geneva, listening to the lectures of Dr. Kraemer, one of the pioneers in the field, and having fellowship with ecumenists from other parts of the world. Much progress has been made in this field since I arrived in America, and I have no doubt about its future growth, if not for idealistic reasons, then for reasons of economy. To give concrete expression to my commitment to ecumenism, I saw to it that all three of the churches I served became members of city, state, national and international ecumenical councils and contributed to their budgets. One of the last satisfactions in this field, before I became a Quaker, was my participation in the merger between the Congregationalists and the Evangelical Reformed, resulting in the United Church of Christ.

Mention should be made of the age-old struggle about the divinity of Jesus. Could anything be more fruitless than the councils that have sat and the centuries that have been wasted in an attempt to establish the extent to which Jesus was divine! Was he "God of Very God", as the Nicene creed has it? Was he a God-man or perhaps just an inspired leader? By what criteria does one establish the degree of divinity in any human being? Certainly not by some peculiar origin of birth in violation of natural law, or on the basis of ancestry. If it has to be done, perhaps a more valid principle would be the degree of sensitivity, the degree of love and compassion exercised by the individual during his lifetime. An appropriate response to this question was once given by an old theological professor who, when confronted by one of his students accusing him of denying the divinity of Jesus, responded by saying, "Young man, I don't deny the divinity of any human being." Yet the question is far from being settled and the argument continues. We can only be grateful that we live in an age when we can no longer be persecuted or burned at the stake for questioning this affirmation of the dogmatists.

Need we mention the mutilations that have been inflicted on one of the most meaningful sacraments, that of Holy Communion? After endless wranglings over con-substantiation and transubstantiation, and all of the other distortions, some Christians still won't sit next to a disciple from another denomination to share in this meaningful tradition. Only the other day, an American Catholic bishop was reprimanded by Rome for being too lenient in this area! That strikes me as reprehensible within the Christian context. What a mockery this makes of the original sacred experience. Here was Jesus, doing what any one of us might do, or has done, when faced with an important decision. Realising the danger to his life, Jesus wanted to be with those whom he loved and with whom he had shared so much, to gain strength and support for the morrow. So he invited his friends to a final meal to celebrate what they had meant to each other. Yet even this simple event could not escape the desecration of minds unfit for spiritual fellowship.

And what of Trinitarianism versus Unitarianism? Fortunately this too was invented long after Jesus and his generation were gone and could not be used as a stumbling block for his disciples. It must be obvious that this argument, as with so many others in the history of Christianity, has nothing to do with living a creative and meaningful life, and has no business being used as a test of discipleship. But they have used it, and many still do; woe unto you if you don't believe in the Trinity. Minds in search of material for the further fragmentation of the Christian family could not overlook these juicy morsels of theology. These are only some of the endless variety of millstones hung about the neck of a people in search of freedom and light. And so religion, which was hopefully to become one of the great reconcilers and means for the unification of the human family, has so often been turned into another means of cruelty and fragmentation. Is it any wonder that so many have had to go to other sources to find an answer to their spiritual hunger?

Let me conclude this section with a summary statement about the Old and the New Testament. I am convinced that no one treating the Bible as The Verbally Inspired Word of God has ever sat down and read it through as we do with countless other books. How anyone could condone the inhumanities and crimes committed, usually against innocent people, in the name of the Old Testament Jehovah, defies moral judgement and a sensitive conscience. There are few crimes that have not been committed without the specific instruction or approval of this ancient deity. We need not mention the inconsistencies, the contradictions and all the other evidences that indicate that this could never be used as a reliable record of history, let alone as the verbally inspired word of God. In the early part of the Old Testament, any cruelty seemed justified when directed toward the non-Jewish outsider. The fingers of the priests dripped with the sacrifical blood of animals, while the swords of the military were stained with the blood of an ancient people that had occupied this territory for a thousand years before the Hebrews came. It was their native home, their cattle and their fields that were being destroyed or confiscated. Their crime consisted of living in an area which Jehovah, quite unexpectedly, offered to the Hebrews, who had just emerged from Egypt. I have often wondered why someone has not suggested that we remember, in addition to the Passover, the thousands of innocent first-born children of the Egyptian families, who were slaughtered, unbelievably, by angels sent by God, to soften the heart of the Pharoah. What are we to make of a religion that would not only condone this evil, but glory in it? Where does that leave fairness, compassion, justice and civility?

There is very little humanitarianism in the Scriptures until we get to that incredible cluster of individuals known as the prophets in the seventh century B.C. This is a phenomenon without parallel in anitiquity. Here we have individuals with a sense of ethical universalism, a sense of justice and fairness, and dreamers of a world reconciled and at peace. These were the true transcendentalists, rising far above the legends, mythologies and cruelty of the earlier centuries of Biblical history. Their sensitivity and vision has had a profound effect upon Western civilization. We are all indebted to them. They will continue to light the way humanity must go if the peaceable kingdom is ever to become a reality. It is here that we can speak of "the inspired word of God," but never as it has been applied to the entire Bible. Furthermore, the Bible makes no claim to infallibility; that was invented by a monk centuries later.

I see the Bible, first of all, as a collection of a great variety of literature, which had its origin long before the Hebrews had a written language. Much of the early beginnings of mythology and legends were collected from more ancient civilizations and transmitted orally for many generations. When the Jews were able to develop a written language, some of these tales of antiquity were recorded. In time it became a book of the history of the Hebrew people, recording the story of a slowly evolving segment of the human family, from slavery to barbarism to civilization and culture. It contains an interesting variety of literature, from mythology to folklore, biography, history, poetry, drama and law. There is no evidence among the early Jews of any scientific discoveries as is true of the Chinese, the Egyptians and the Greeks. Its major contribution consists of the slow sensitization of the human conscience which, in time, culminated in the wisdom of the prophets. I believe that the lyric poetry of the psalms is among the greatest poetry of antiquity. Even some of these are tainted by arrogance, self-righteousness and national pride, and one has to be careful when making a choice for liturgical purposes or personal inspiration. Here and there we come upon a crumb of wisdom and spiritual insight. Jesus treated some of its crude moral insight with, *It has been told you of old, but I tell you.* He was in touch with a nobler source of moral insight and challenged his followers to rise above the Old Testament. Growth and progress required that the individual go beyond what was sacred in the past to become worthy of a new age. It is morally indefensible to condone the cruelties of the Old Testament indiscriminately, whether they were ordered by Jehovah or anyone else. We cannot apply one standard of morality in judging the Scriptures and another for non-Biblical history. The Bible is not the word of God, but it contains a rare amount of spiritual insight.

In the New Testament we are in the presence of a new conception of life. When Jesus spoke of the Fatherhood of God, he lifted the God-concept far beyond the nationalistic religions of the past. And when he spoke of neighborliness, he insisted that it must be without horizons and include every creature in need of compassion. What we have in the Gospels is not a true picture of Jesus, but a reflection of what each of the evangelists saw in him. Mark, with the least amount of education and almost a child-like style of writing, was the first one to report. Matthew, as a devout Jew, must be read more carefully, for he writes with the purpose of trying to prove that Jesus was the fulfillment of the Old Testament. His constantly repeated phrase is that this happened "that it be fulfilled what had been spoken by the prophets." Luke is the Gospel that I like best. He, a well-educated Greek physician, has the most beautiful style and, because of his sensitivity to suffering as a doctor, tells us a number of stories that the others overlooked. John can hardly be used as biographical material. His Gospel lends itself best to devotional use. It is an exercise in the Greek Logos philosophy which John had learned from the Greek philosopher Philo.

The letters of Paul and the book of Acts written by Luke are the only early information we have about the spread of Christianity and the problems the young movement faced in confronting the gentile world. It would have been best if the book of Revelations had never been included in the Biblical canon. It is an exercise in near Eastern symbology, used to express the conviction that the new faith would ultimately triumph. No book in the Bible has lent itself to more distortions by preachers who know nothing of Eastern pantheons and symbolism. The ultimate refinement of Biblical insight and its essence I find expressed in the Sermon on the Mount, which, for me, is one of the noblest expressions of a sensitive soul that has found its home in God.

Chapter 16

THEOLOGY: FUNDAMENTALISM

My mother was a vivacious, imaginative and attractive person, with a delightful sense of humour, who loved her husband and her children. She was outgoing and one of the most generous individuals I have known. She liked beautiful dresses, yet the only clothing she ever wore was made by herself or with the help of a friend. Among these I remember especially a dress made of white silk with tiny flowers on it, a piece of material given her by a friend. I don't remember ever mentioning this to her, but for my childhood taste, it was the most beautiful dress she ever had, standing in dramatic contrast to her raven black hair and dark eyes. I don't believe that her youthful charm lasted very long under the conditions under which she had to live. Married at seventeen, she must have gotten pregnant the night of the wedding. She gave birth to sixteen children. I have the impression that she was pregnant for thirty years. And one has to keep in mind where and under what conditions these children were born – from Poland to Siberia to the Ukraine, England and finally Canada. On one of my visits to Canada as a student, when I found her pregnant again, I could not restrain myself and spoke to her about it. But before I was able to get out of the house, the message had gotten to father, who called me into his study and asked how I could dare to criticize my parents and the laws of God established in the Bible. I never mentioned the subject again, but I resolved, on my way back to Rochester, never to have any children of my own. I felt that there should be more to life for a woman than an endless pregnancy, ordained by some ancient superstition.

Not until years later did the results of an irrational human fecundity reach the consciousness of social scientists. The first book that made clear to me what was being done to the earth, to our resources, and to our supply of food, was entitled *Our Plundered Planet*. Until then my reaction to overbreeding was purely on the basis of what it did to the mother and its effect on poverty. Now I had scientific evidence of the crime that was being committed against nature itself. Since my coming to the U.S. the population of the world has increased by three billion more humans. By the end of this century there will be six billion occupying the same planet. This, not the atom bomb, is the greatest threat to man's survival. Millions are starving already. And what is almost beyond comprehension to me is how the Catholic hierarchy, starting with the Pope, can maintain a pre-medieval position in the face of this threat to any kind of meaningful life, while condemning countless millions to a life of poverty and slow starvation. Looking at such facts, I am inclined to agree with George Bernard Shaw that the church has been one of the greatest stumbling blocks to human progress, usually supporting some antiquated tradition, incapable of responding creatively to new demands. The insistence on procreation is a revolt against reason. I recently observed a television scene during the Pope's visit to Africa which will remain etched in my memory. This was a huge out-of-door meeting, with people standing, sitting or lying on the ground. Below the podium from which the Pope was speaking, sat a poorly-clad mother with five or six naked children crawling over her body like ants. Meanwhile, the Pope, above her, was again expounding the medieval notion of divine law which forbids the use of contraceptives for the regulation of the size of the family. This may well have been inspired by words from Pope Pius, who was in turn inspired by words from St. Augustine. He called it a "sin against nature" and a "deed shameful and intrinsically wicked." Here was a scene crying for pity, mercy and under-standing. What future was there for these little wretches on a planet over-whelmed by human reproduction? Fortunately many of my Catholic friends get their direction from a higher law, suited to the conditions and demands of contemporary life. So far, only China is taking this threat to human survival seriously and is getting significant results. I recently had an opportunity to take a close look at their concern for human welfare. I have taken this threat so seriously that I required of the many couples who came to me to be married, that if there was any indication that they were not sufficiently informed about birth control, that they visit a Planned Parenthood Clinic before they came for a second visit. Literature on this subject was always available in my office.

But let us return to my parents, who were deeply in love and devoted to each other. No harsh word ever passed between them. Sex and reproduction, as with so many other things in my father's life, were regulated by the Bible. Father seemed to have a text for almost anything, and if there were a text for it there was no point in questioning it. I will quote a paragraph from a letter I received from my brother Bill in Canada. He grew up after I had left the family and knew the parents in their later years. He wrote, "I have never known my parents to be abusive or unfair. They were generous in their poverty. Many a tramp and others have knocked on our door, and no one was ever turned away for either a piece of bread or a night's lodging. In Canada they maintained a little box with a slot on top. Below the lid were inscribed the words from Malachi 3:10. The first ten cents of every dollar that stopped at our home went into that box, and then either found its way to church on Sunday or into the hands of some charitable enterprise. They had so little that once a letter had to be held up because there was not enough to buy a three cent stamp...".

The work my mother had to do each day, from early morning until late at night, would be difficult to comprehend by anyone born into our gadget-oriented civilization. She had a much more inquisitive nature than father, and I am grateful that my genetic inheritance was dominated by my mother's genes.

I can still see her in Siberia, after a long day's grueling toil, opening a large volume on human history, reading a few pages with the book on her lap, and then falling asleep. How this book ever found its way into our home is a mystery to me. But when I recall that picture today, of mother bending over that heavy volume, it tells me a great deal about her nature. I doubt very much that she ever got beyond the first chapter during those five years in Siberia, but what I admire and appreciate is that mother must have had a longing to find out where and when man's long history began, and the road over which he has travelled. Father, if he ever raised these questions at all, found the answer in the book of Genesis, and no Darwinian theory or anthropology could shed any light on that Biblical scene. Mother, like father, was completely without formal education beyond the fourth grade, yet she could read and write a letter.

She was the incarnation of kindness, helping wherever she could, even if it meant depriving her own family of some of the necessities. How we older children used to fight over the privilege of taking a piece of cake or a loaf of bread at Christmas or Eastertime to a family in the village who, mother explained to us, was poorer than we were. She told me during my last visit to Canada before she died, that she and dad had managed to send some eighty packages to Europe after the last war. When I asked her where she found the $800.00 it took to send these gifts, she just smiled. They remained true to the vow they made the day they were married, when they promised God that they would use a tenth of their income to assist others. And I can vouch that this covenant was never broken, no matter how precarious life sometimes became.

My father was a theological fundamentalist and Biblical literalist, but fortunately not of the intolerable variety we find in America. Having had to go to work when he was nine years old in order to get food for himself, as his parents were too poor to feed the entire family, he also had no chance for a formal education. He was able to attend classes a few times in the winter, but I doubt whether he ever got to the fourth grade. Whatever he became beyond that level he had to achieve on his own. At thirteen he became an apprentice and at sixteen he qualified for the weaving profession.

He too was by nature a kindly person, outgoing and compassionate. He had no managerial ability, which placed the burden of managing the large family completely on mother's shoulders. He seems to have had little anxiety about the future, no matter how difficult life became. His answer was always that God would provide for us. When I once asked him why God would care for us while others were starving and often dying, he quietly looked at me as if I were too young to understand this discriminatory theology. After serving for four years in the Russian army, he returned home to his weaving stool. But one of the beloved German Baptist ministers in Poland must have recognized a potential in father of which he himself was unaware. Reverend Alf decided to groom father for the ministry. Consequently, father slowly moved off the weaving bench and behind the pulpit.

People loved and respected father so that he never had to look for a church. His problem was how to choose between the invitations that came to him, without violating the will of God for his life. When he had to make a difficult choice of that nature, without having his ego interfere with the divine will, he would resort to the drawing of lots. The board of deacons would write the names on slips of paper, drop these into a hat, offer a prayer and then the lot was drawn to determine the next move. The divine election was final. He had done the same thing when, at the age of twenty-six, he decided to marry. There were two eligible maidens in the community, named Maria and Elizabeth. The name pulled out of the hat under divine guidance was Maria. The wedding soon followed, and Maria became my mother. He was totally committed to God, as he conceived him, and to the Christian gospel. Even in Siberia he managed to start a number of churches in some of the outlying villages.

However, true to the fundamentalist tradition, there was only one true faith, one true theology and one Biblical interpretation, and that was father's. How could I forget my disappointment and pain when, upon graduating from the academy with honors, I went home for a visit to tell my parents about my achievements. During the first meal the conversation drifted in the direction of religion and theology. Father soon detected that I was no longer using the familiar terminology, nor had I returned with the beliefs I had when I left four years earlier. Here I was feeling that I had overcome insurmountable barriers and had worked myself almost to a mental breakdown, and father expected my religion to have remained untouched, as ignorant and uninformed as before. I assume that it had been taken for granted that I would know something about history, physics, chemistry, astronomy, literature and the rest, but in religion I was not to have picked up a single new idea. After that painful encounter, I decided never again to discuss religion with my father. What a pity it seemed to me, that here we were, two ministers, with the door on theology shut between us. During those years I had discovered an entirely new universe -- the world of art, science, literature and ideas. I had discovered a new meaning to life that I did not previously know existed. My religious enjoyment of life had taken on ever enlarging dimensions, yet I was not expected to make any mention of this. This refusal to allow the mind to be as creative in religion as in any other department of life has been one of the curses of mankind, not only in the Catholic church, but also in many Protestant churches. Only a liberal Protestantism has been able to leave behind this crippling hold on the human mind, while Catholicism and fundamentalism persist in their anti-intellectualism.

What surprises me is that most of the rest of the family has retained much of the theology of our father. Only one of my brothers, who was a professor of philosophy at a Catholic university in Canada, and I had a remarkable rapport in our thinking. I and another of my brothers, who visited me some time ago, began to discuss religion on the day he was to leave. While holding my hand as we were saying good-bye, he concluded the visit by saying, "If this is what education has done to you, I am glad I never went to school." Here is a man who lives in a comfortable home, with all the convenience modern industry makes possible, and who has had a triple bypass through heart surgery, all the result of an enormous amount of education, research and scientific achievement! It is learning that has made our civilization possible, yet when it comes to religion, this phase of life has to remain untouched and any new ideas remain suspect.

The Lutherans had gotten to Poland and Russia before the Baptists arrived and gave father a great deal of trouble. Since no Protestant could be buried in a Greek Orthodox cemetery, and since many of the Baptist churches were still without cemeteries, they had to be buried with the Lutherans, if the Lutherans did not lock the gates. If the Lutherans refused to grant permission, the corpse sometimes had to be buried outside the fence. Once, in the case of the death of a child, father and his deacons took the child for burial but found the cemetery gate guarded by a number of Lutherans. Refused permission to enter, they decided to leave the casket at the gate and hid in a forest nearby to see what the Lutherans would do. After a lengthy debate they buried the child, for they knew that they would be held responsible if the child, according to law, was not buried within three days. On another occasion, when father knew in advance that he was facing a similar problem, he secured a contingent of cossack soldiers on horses, who saw to it that there would be no interference.

In contrast to these humanitarian acts, my father's preaching, as far as I can remember, had little to do with the redemption of life here on earth. It contained no criticism or revolt against the brutalising conditions under which most of humanity had to live. The social gospel never got to Russia or Poland. There was no prophetic vision against injustice and abuse. It was the business of religion to convert people and save them from going to hell, which was everyone's destiny whose life had not been changed by the Gospel. It was a theology based on the forgiveness of sin and of the promise of a better life beyond the stars. Having spent one Sunday afternoon with the staff of Dr. Orlof's Baptist church in Moscow in 1966, I realized that whatever changes may have taken place in Russia since we left the country, they have had little effect on Baptist theology. Neither has the Greek Orthodox Church of Russia wavered for a thousand years from its course. The book on church history presented to me by Metropolitan Nikoli of Moscow states on the second page that "it is the purpose of the church to prepare souls for eternity".

Coming out of this background of fundamentalism into which no new light was permitted to penetrate, it would be difficult for anyone who has not gone this lonesome journey, to appreciate the intellectual struggle I had to endure, as my mind slowly awoke from its illiterate slumber and discovered the grandeur of creation and the potential of the mind. As I look back on that past now, it seems to me that the main reason for my difficulty had its origin in the tension created by an insatiable mind and the fundamentalist ideas deposited deep in my subconscious during the years of my childhood. While the mind was free to wing its way through an unobstructed universe and rejoice over every new discovery, the subconscious could not be brought into line. In time the two do arrive at the same level, but we must be willing to wait. Only after this harmonization has taken place can we begin to function as wholesome, integrated personalities. Here I want to mention only a few identifiable events that fueled the struggle, and broke down the walls of fundamentalism.

It began at first quite harmlessly. I no longer remember for what reason but one of the professors, shortly after our arrival in Rochester, asked us to take three different coloured pencils, make a map of Palestine and trace the movements of Jesus according to the first three Gospels. I do not know what, if anything, this meant to my classmates, for they were surprised that I should be so upset. But for me it was the first blow against the notion that the Bible is the infallible verbally inspired word of God. If this was true, why was there such discrepancy in regards to the movements of Jesus on the map? Some time later came the comparison between the genealogies of Matthew and Luke, both ending in a Virgin Birth. Not only are the genealogies radically different, but the non-biological conclusion nullified the original effort. What did this do to the verbal inspiration? While all of this fermentation was going on in my mind, I was taking a walk through Highland Park and passed one of the library windows at Colgate Rochester Divinity School. In the window was a display of the Code of Hammurabi and the Ten Commandments by Moses, supposed to have been written by the finger of God. To my surprise I noticed that some of the Commandments were verbatim copies of the Code of Hammurabi, who lived centuries before Moses. Plagiarism, I thought at first! What if some of the rest of the material in the Old Testament was also garnered from earlier sources? Not until later, when we studied Assyrian and Babylonian civilizations did I discover that considerable additional material had been copied from more ancient sources and ascribed to the Hebrew Jehovah.

Now, in retrospect, why should this discovery have been such a blow to my childhood training? First of all because it violated my cozy acceptance of the Bible as the word of God, an absurdity which is still being propagated by a numberless army of pulpiteers and transmitted to millions of unthinking devotees. Secondly, I was still worshipping the national deity of Judaism, a fanatic Jewish God. And such a God would have nothing to do with a pagan Hammurabi, who had received his code of laws from the god Shamash. It was this religious nationalism that provided the basis for the Hebrew destruction of a defenseless people in Palestine. Not only were countless human beings exterminated in the name of the God of Moses, but a whole civilization that had been in existence more than a thousand years before the Jews arrived. Only when we arrive at the point of worshipping the

God of humanity can we appreciate why a Hammurabi should be numbered among the children of God. And there should be no problem believing that God could use him in the revelation of new moral insight, as well as anyone else. It took a long and painful process to grope my way through these ruins of Biblical literalism and religious nationalism to a universalism that set no limits to God, and in which there are no chosen people who deserve preferential treatment.

The next, and perhaps the most devastating blow to my biblically constructed universe, did not come from the Bible, but from geometry of all places. Mathematics had been one of the most difficult ordeals for me, since I had absolutely no background for it. At this time I had not even seen a multiplication table. Yet I had to move along with the rest of the class and keep on memorizing each day new rules and formulas. Yet there was something even then about this subject that fascinated me. It seemed to give evidence of orderliness and reliability; it was an insight based on empirical evidence. But one day, in preparation for class, I came upon something that stopped me cold in my tracks. It had to do with a formula that stated that if one stood at the shore of a river and selected two points on one side and a third point at the opposite side of the river, one could determine the width of the river without ever crossing it. I was so struck by this new phenomenon that tears came to my cheeks. I read the paragraph again and again, while the realization grew that if this was true in Rochester, it had to be true anywhere in the universe. Hence this must be a dependable universe, not a creation of a capricious deity. In such a law-abiding universe, people do not walk on water, as the Bible maintains; axes do not float because an Old Testament priest prays over them. The sun could not be made to stand still so that an enraged Joshua, as a tool in the hands of God, would have time enough to exterminate every living thing in the city of Jericho, every innocent mother, child and beast. If this was true, then Elijah could not take off for heaven on a chariot drawn by a team of horses, nor could a woman have been constructed out of a man's rib. Nor was it likely that a person could be resurrected from the grave to join his friends for a fishfry. No, in a law-abiding universe such things could not happen.

That afternoon I went to my geometry class in a daze, unable to believe what I had just read. While the professor lectured, my mind was spinning infinite yarns of deduction while a deep joy pervaded my soul. My mind had touched the hem of an orderly and dependable universe, based upon laws that could not be violated by either God or man; laws that could be trusted and utilized for the benefit of mankind. The chaotic world of the Bible, where angels could rearrange the furniture at will, had met its death knell. I was beginning to feel at home in the new world I had discovered. One of the reasons, no doubt, why this seemed to me so important at that time, may have been because of the uncertainties and the precariousness and dangers that had always hung over my family and childhood. Nothing had seemed reliable and safe; there were no anchors to cling to, only an unpredictable universe. To this day I have never been evicted from my newly discovered intellectual home.

Another subject that helped to put the world in order for me was a course in astronomy. Since I had never seen a map of the earth or the heavens, mine was still the Biblical three-layer cake kind of a world, with a flat earth in the middle, a heaven above and a hell below. Everything was permanently fixed in the center of creation. Even as a child, I already had some doubts about a flood somewhere in Palestine that was said to have covered the whole earth and drowned every living thing. It was difficult for me to see where they, whoever was doing this, could have found enough water to get all the way to Siberia. I also had some reservations about a man called Noah, who was supposed to have been able to build an ark, long before there were nails and steel beams; an ark big enough to house seven pairs of each form of life, or even one pair, according to the sceptic who rewrote the story in the Bible. It was the Ptolemaic cosmology that took care of my flat earth and rounded it into a sphere. It was the great Copernicus who set the earth in motion, removed it from the center of creation and made it spin around its solar system. One of my deep sorrows came when I discovered many years later that the Catholic church had tortured the soul out of the great scientist, Galileo, for disturbing its monolithic theology that required that the earth be left in its immovable place. I am pleased to see that the church has finally gotten around to reinstating the man, implying that he may have been right! All of these discoveries were most helpful, but there was much more to come, before I could take my place in a creation that was not alien to human life; a universe to which man rightly belonged and in which he could find happiness without irrational threats from beyond.

Another problem that gave me some difficulty was the question of ethics. There came a time when my simple code of ethics, by which I had lived as a child, no longer sufficed. My code simply consisted of not doing anything that would bring harm to others or myself, and to do that which gave me pleasure and which I could afford. But there came a time when moral decisions had to be made that were far too complex for this simple moral code. I was now in need of a criterion that was as reliable as the laws of geometry and as universally applicable. The Jesus I knew then had not yet been raised to the stature of a great historical figure and a source of moral insight. I still saw him as a miracle worker, shrouded in other-worldliness and of little consequence for daily life. Hence I had to look for my answer in other directions. What first came to my rescue was something I read in Immanuel Kant, who said that human beings must never be used as means to an end, but always as ends in themselves. And that we must always act from a principle which could be turned into a universal law. This said to me that we must always act from a principle that had universal application. This was moving in the right direction, but left me still unsatisfied. Next came a sermon by Harry Emerson Fosdick, "How to Tell Right From Wrong", who by that time had become for me the dean of American preachers. This clarified the issue further, but it was not until I discovered Dr. Albert Schweitzer, that I knew that I had discovered the ultimate moral principle.

Dr. Schweitzer had been searching for years for an ethical principle by which he could explain the rise and fall of civilizations. While making his way on a boat one day on the Ogobe River in Africa, moving slowly through a herd of hippopotamuses, the answer suddenly came -- *Ehrfurcht vor dem Leben, or Reverence for Life.* I knew instantly that I had found the answer to my search.

How grateful I was for this discovery. Here was a universally valid moral principle that applied not only to relations between human beings, but also to every form of life, no matter how low on the evolutionary scale, and even embraced the world of nature. No one in the Western world has carried this principle to its ultimate conclusion as has Schweitzer. This is his summary of its ultimate application:

That man is truly ethical who shatters no ice crystal as it sparkles in the sun, tears no leaf from a tree, cuts no flowers... The farmer who has mown down a thousand flowers in his meadow to feed his cows, must be careful on his way home not to strike off in heedless pastime the head of a single flower by the roadside for he thereby commits a wrong against life without being under the pressure of necessity.

This is ultimate, and of such quality that I doubt that it shall ever be surpassed. I don't think that humanity will ever find anything more valid. It became for me the guiding beacon of my life. In time this principle sank deeper and deeper into my being, until the witness of suffering on the part of any form of life or nature became a painful experience. I came to feel with Schweitzer that, "As long as living creatures suffer, there is no possibility of joy for those who are full of compassion". I am inclined to think that this ethical criterion must have been the basis upon which Jesus made his moral decisions. Here is a principle that looks upon every form of creation as sacred. If we continue to hope for redemption of life on our planet, we will have to come to the acceptance of this principle for human behavior.

Chapter 17

AMERICA

I feel that I should also say something about America, the country to which I owe so much for having made possible the life I have been privileged to live. It is here where the deepest satisfactions and rewards of my life have been born. When my English had developed sufficiently, so that I was able to begin reading some of the great humanistic documents of our statesmen, I was profoundly impressed by the idealism expressed in the Preamble to the Constitution; by the Bill of Rights; by some of the speeches of Woodrow Wilson; and by the words of Lincoln. I found it difficult to believe that such idealism could have found its way into the national documents of a people. Against my background, this was more than I had a right to expect from history. Who can read, without being deeply moved, these magnificent words from Lincoln's Second Inaugural. They represent a depth of spiritual refinement and nobility unknown in political documents. "With malice toward none; with charity for all; with firmness in the rights as God gives us the light to see the right, let us strive on to finish the work we are in; to bind up the nation's wounds; to care for him who shall have borne the battle, and for his widow, and his orphan -- to do all which may achieve and cherish a just and lasting peace among ourselves, and with all nations." One must read the rest of this speech to get the full impact of these noble words. Here we have a sentiment that surpasses Isaiah and Jeremiah, and represents the best in Christianity.

But as I kept on reading and came to know American society from personal participation in it, the vision soon faded. How could millions of our children in school repeat each day in the Pledge of Allegiance, "...with liberty and justice for all," while their parents had no intention of seeing that these ideas became implemented in the life and blood of the nation? How was it possible that in a democracy, some of the companions in my car could not join me in a restaurant? I had to buy the sandwiches and we ate them along the road. How could an intelligent and educated people make such a mockery out of what they professed? We had a greater honesty, trust and equality among the natives of Siberia. More and more I came to know the mockery that had been made of our national documents. After I became a citizen, having to live with my conscience, I resolved that I would do what I could in my brief lifetime to rectify some of the injustice and ease the burden of humanity. To this day I have identified with the blacks and with other underprivileged members of society. And they, in turn, have made their contribution to and enriched my life.

A speech that I have been asked to give many times is entitled *Undimmed by Human Tears*. In these simple words I saw embedded all the idealism that went into the founding of this nation and the vision of its future. We must not rest until every child is properly dressed, every sickness cared for, every citizen properly educated, every person housed, and every one who can work employed. The other day it struck me as an obscenity when I read in the Wall Street Journal the names of our contemporary billionaires; this in the face of the homeless and the hungry, and the dehumanising conditions under which millions in our nation have to live. This is a further indication of our moral depravity, and the extent to which we ridicule the idealism of the founders of this nation. I was invited by the dean of the Episcopal Cathedral in Baltimore to give this address in connection with the nation's observance of the bicentennial. It has since been published in a book commemorating the event.

There is little one person can do in the face of such universal evil. But in order to maintain my integrity I had to become involved, and to join other people who were determined to improve conditions for others. For me it began at Oberlin, where we discovered that blacks were not allowed into the barbershops. Some of the reasons given were that they would lose their white clients and that they would have difficulty cutting kinky hair. When we failed in our attempt to open the shops for all citizens, we raised the money, rented a room, and engaged a charming and gallant young fellow from Jamaica, who could cut anyone's hair in just a few minutes. Students and others soon flocked to his barbership, and before long every barber in town had learned to cut kinky hair. While the deacons of my churches never stood at my side when I demonstrated for open housing, stood vigil at the rotunda of the state capital in Topeka or attempted to find jobs for discharged prisoners, they never interfered with my efforts. They allowed me the freedom to do what my conscience demanded of me. It was different when I arrived in Baltimore, where the Quakers and others had been marching on Washington in great numbers, expressing their opposition to the war in Vietnam, our policies in South Africa, and the conduct of the CIA and the government in Central America. Here I was no longer alone, and we walked shoulder to shoulder. These efforts have not been in vain. Vietnam was evacuated. There is a heightened consciousness in parts of the nation. The lot of the blacks has been improving and some injustices have been outlawed by the courts. But the struggle must continue; a great deal more needs to be done, especially in the area of economic justice.

On one of the visits to Russia I took a long walk one night along the Volga with a professor. It was an unforgettable evening since in a short while over a cup of tea, we had suddenly recognized a deep affinity between us. Our conversation touched on many subjects. Sometime during that evening the professor said: "You come from a Christian country, yet you hold the world's record of broken homes, you lead the world in crime and homicides, you have many undernourished children and homeless people, you have millions of unemployed, you have more illegitimate children than any other nation. We are supposed to be an atheistic country, yet our government sees to it that everyone has a job, and in spite of the billions of dollars of destruction during the last war, the government sees to it that every citizen has a shelter. We have little crime, and we provide a free education and health care for everyone. Why should we become a Christian nation?" Instead of attempting an answer, I changed the subject.

The following night, when I returned to my hotel, I found the lobby crowded to the last foot of space. I could not imagine what might have happened. But as I made my way with great difficulty to the stairs, I realized that this was the only floor with a TV. And on the screen I saw a picture familiar to all of us. They were showing one of the civil rights marches in Alabama. It was the scene where the bloodhounds of Bull Conner were tearing at human beings and the police were beating them to the ground with clubs, while the fire hoses were rolling people across the street like matchsticks. As the scene faded a neatly dressed man came on the screen to explain to the audience what they had just seen. This, he said, is what America does to those citizens who are demanding their human rights, and much more. One has to see this on a Russian screen to be able to take in the full depravity of it. That night I tried to get to my room as fast as possible, before anyone could identify me as an American. Can anyone imagine what this must say to a people who have so little information about this nation?

Yet this has become a nation that is interfering with foreign governments all over the globe, either through the CIA or by military intervention. What business do we have imposing our morally bankrupt system on any people before we learn to build a more humane and just society at home? By the time we get through plundering the planet with our insatiable industrial and consumer demands, what will be left will be ripe for Communism anywhere. Communism finds its richest soil in places where hunger and hopelessness have prepared the way. Having taken a close look at China recently, where millions have had to starve over the centuries, and now everyone has his bowl of rice, it becomes obvious that a highly disciplined society is capable of accomplishing what we are incapable of doing ourselves.

America arrived a bit late on the international scene, when the other empire builders, such as England, Spain, Holland and France, were already on the decline. Yet we seem to be determined to keep the embers of a modified imperialism glowing a while longer. It is a pity that we are either ill-informed or insensitive to history; that we are incapable of seeing the consequences of our political and military behavior abroad. In Vietnam, for example, we not only inflicted incalculable suffering on a civilian population, but we destroyed an entire ancient civilization, ten thousand miles away from our shores. And for what purpose? To mention only a few of the tyrants with whom we have been doing business and whose partnership we cultivated, we can begin with

Chiang Kai Shek of China, the Shah of Iran, Marcos of the Phillipines, Franco of Spain, and their ilk in many other places. At Heidelberg University I finally had to give up trying to explain and defend the conduct of American foreign policy to groups of students who did not know what to make of our policies and our kind of democracy. Since communism feeds on destitution, injustice and helplessness, we are the ones cultivating the soil for its success. Our ignorance of history and of forces that shape the character of a people makes it impossible for us to understand the aspirations of others. Our dealings with Russia give ample evidence of our incompetence. Any wonder that George Kennan, that elder statesman and wise historian, informs us that what we have in the State Department, which determines much of our policy, is *intellectual primitivism?*

Yet if this nation were capable of producing a leadership that was committed to compassion, service and justice, instead of relying on militarism, we could once more become the beacon of light for the "tempest-tossed, yearning to be free." We would not have to resort to assasination and military brutalities to subject others. Part of our insane military budget could be used to feed the hungry, clothe the naked, and bring hope to the destitute, as Jesus commanded. Others would come to us from many places to learn ways of establishing a humane social order on earth. But this hope I have long since had to give up in the face of what we seem determined to do. The only hope I still have for a more just democratic system is what I have observed in some of the western European countries. Here we have examples of fairness and justice actually implemented. Perhaps they can lead the way for others.

When I became an American citizen in the federal court of Cleveland, Ohio, there were eighty of us being sworn in at the same time. I stood in the back row when we were asked to raise our hands to be sworn in. I was impressed by what I saw in front of me. Here were richly diamond-decorated fingers; here were neatly groomed artistic hands; and there were hands gnarled by years of unrelenting toil. Behind the judge was the flag of the nation, unfurled against a mahogany-panelled wall. Tears came to my eyes when I suddenly realized that this is what democracy should be all about. In the presence of the star spangled banner we had suddenly all become equals, no matter what our station in life or our origin. That dream must not be allowed to die. Perhaps future generations, more noble and humane than ours, may become capable of implementing the dream more fully.

Chapter 18

THE QUESTION OF GOD

Finally we arrive at the question of God. This subject was much more difficult and required a great deal more attention. No effort was spared, and my reading covered much of Western as well as Oriental thought. As my universe continued to expand, it soon became evident that my childhood deity was totally inadequate to cope with these new dimensions. The nature of God had to be changed and reinterpreted. Different professors had different interpretations, and the endless theological literature only added to the confusion instead of clarifying the issue. There was too much subjectivism and too little dependable objective evidence. And before the question of the nature of God could be solved, I began to question the whole theory of a dualistic conception of creation. It seems to me that, to date, no convincing evidence has yet been found to prove that the universe is a composite of matter and spirit, of nature and God, and of creator and creation. Especially in recent decades the preponderance of evidence has been moving in the opposite direction. The arguments from cause and effect; the great watchmaker; the telefinalism of Lecomte du Nuoy; and the classic argument by Thomas Aquinas, who tried to prove the existence of God on teleological, cosmological and anthropological grounds, all lost their validity in the universe I saw emerging.

The incredible anthropomorphic notions which have been associated with God ever since our race began and are still dominating the world of religion, seem to me an expression of wishful thinking. They only seem to point at a significant human characteristic: man has a need to cling to something outside of himself. And if there is nothing out there, he feels compelled to create his own deities to fill the vacuum. We are frightened by vast empty spaces and feel compelled to fill them with creations of our own making. They are games played by children without demonstrable substance. In spite of Kant's warning about the unreliability of our metaphysical flights, man persists in clinging to his own creations. A look at the religions of mankind -- where an endless variety of objects, from roots to animals, from mountains to the stars, have been used as objects of worship -- is further evidence of the lack of any empirical objective reality to respond to the metaphysical hunger of the soul. It only demonstrates man's desperate need to transcend himself, and the unreliability of the objects to which he has given his devotion.

What is even more sobering is the realization to what use these devotional loyalties have been put. A look at history gives ample evidence of the role religion has played in the human struggle. Today it is Israel, India, the Near East, Ireland, and other places where conceived and worshipped deities are used to inspire fanaticism and human cruelty. And who can dismiss the religious wars in Europe over the centuries, including the Crusades with their indescribable brutalities against life. Nor do we need to mention America's slavery. I once did some research to find out what was said from the American pulpit during those decades when humans were treated like animals. I was impressed by the ingenuity employed by the clergy to make texts support an economically profitable business! The most cruel wars in history have been fought in the name of some deity, from Joshua to the Ayatollah, both Christian and non-Christian. And if this is not enough, relax in some comfortable chair, turn on the TV or radio, and listen to some of the unbelievable religious nonsense used in the name of some contemporary American deity which pollutes the airwaves. While we may make fun of the theological beliefs of others and claim that ours are better, I have yet to find a single one, no matter what religious absurdity he clings to, who does not believe that his is the true faith!

There is nothing for me in that Babel of voices out there. I have long since, for my own deep joy and satisfaction, arrived at a monistic philosophy of creation and the universe. This means that all existence is constituted out of one substance. Of all the philosophers, the one that comes closest to my position is Spinoza, the *God-intoxicated Jew*. He wrote centuries ago that "God and substance are the same and constitute the eternal order of the world..." There is here no traditional line of demarcation between matter and spirit, nor is there a distinction between body and mind or soma and psyche. They are both attributes of the same reality. To endow God with human traits and purposes is an anthropomorphic delusion, like so much of our religious thinking. Such practice is the result of an erroneous homocentric view of creation, instead of viewing it cosmocentrically. We project into the universe our own little microcosms and hope that God will oblige us by adjusting his world to our own temporary whims. I do not know to what extent this position is supported by the rest of the philosophic world, but I have found a compatriot among the Greeks who lived some three thousand years ago, by the name of Thales, who may have been the first. But I do know that my support is growing rapidly in the world of scientific research.

The material elements constituting the universe are capable of an infinite variety of combinations and forms, from the simplest to the most complex, from plant to self-conscious life. Matter, mind, intelligence and will are all manifestations or, to use Spinoza's term, *attributes, of the same reality*. There is no reason or need for an influence from beyond, nor do we need to look for some special immanent reality. The traditional notion of God becomes a part of the incredible mystery of creation, instead of being a force imposed on it from without. Einstein, for a lifetime, had been in search of the unifying principle. He never found it, but I am satisfied that sooner or later, like a Schweitzer in search of the ultimate ethical principle, someone will stumble on it, and the mystery will become clear. Looking at the report of a recent international conference of physicists they concluded that energy is the basis of all reality. It is the concentration of energy that turns into particles of matter which, in turn, provide the basis for all forms of empirical existence. The search continues and perhaps someday may result in a harmonious concept of the universe, and the basis of it will be monistic. A recent book that throws some light on this search is *The Tao of Physics* by the physicist Fritjof Capra. Much more needs to be done and is being done in many laboratories around the world.

For myself, I am already completely at home in my monistic universe. I have found my peace, my tranquility, and no longer have to wait for further evidence. Should anyone think unkindly of me for having come to this conclusion, it is good to remember that we do not choose our *Weltanschauung*. We may choose our profession, where we are going to live, or whom we are going to marry, but we cannot choose our ultimate convictions. Over these we have no control. These are the result of the sum total of experiences that impinge on our being. By some mysterious process of assimilation they become synthesized and determine our point of view. Not to accept the result and try to live accordingly, would be in violation of our integrity. This is who we have become and who we are. That is why Socrates, rather than save his life by following the advice of his friends, took the hemlock. That is why Luther, standing before the Diet at Worms declared, "Here I stand, so help me God, I can do no otherwise." And that is why Erasmus insisted, "I cannot do other than what I am." This is the process by which I have arrived at monism. In the light of what I know, this is the only position that makes sense to me. There may be more out there that think the way I do, but whether there are or not, their number will increase in the century to come.

Since I arrived at this point of view, most of the chaos has vanished. I am finding the universe, especially nature, a far more interesting and mysterious creation. I stand in awe of the incredible inventiveness of nature, from the tiniest insect to the giants of the African veldt. What Einstein has to say on this subject is something to which my soul responds with joy. Let me quote a paragraph from one of his books. *The most beautiful thing we can experience is the mysterious. It is the source of all true art and science. He to whom this emotion is a stranger, who can no longer pause to wonder and stand wrapped in awe, is as good as dead; his eyes are closed. This insight into the mystery of life... has also given rise to religion. To know that what is impenetrable to us really exists, manifesting itself as the highest wisdom or the most radiant beauty which our dull faculties can comprehend only in their most primitve forms -- this knowledge, this feeling is at the center of all true religiousness. In this sense, and in this sense alone, I belong to the rank of devoutly religious men. We are all children of that mystery.*

I prefer not to use the traditional symbol of God any more, since no one knows what is meant by it, and every one has his private interpretation. Furthermore, it has been and still is the basis of the most unbelievable distortions of history, life and reality. The writings of theologians have lost their meaning for me, since much of what they have to say is based on syllogisms of which the premises are undemonstrable. To quote Einstein again, "I cannot imagine a God who rewards and punishes the objects of his creation, whose purposes are modeled after our own -- a God, in short, who is but a reflection of human frailty. Neither can I believe that the individual survives the death of his body, although feeble souls harbor such thoughts through fear or religious egotism. It is enough for me to contemplate the mystery of conscious life... to reflect upon the marvelous structure of the universe which we can dimly perceive, and to try humbly to comprehend even an infinitesimal part of the intelligence manifested in nature."

My present orientation has not robbed me of any of the joy and enrichment I find in worship with other fellow creatures. One does not need the symbol of a deity in order to worship. There are many reasons for worship and celebration. Every Sunday finds me worshipping in one of the churches of different denominations, or in a silent Quaker meeting. Worship, for me, means to celebrate my existence and the grandeur and mystery of the world which surrounds me. The loss of my childhood deity has only enhanced my mystical experience. Perhaps this is what Bonhoeffer, the promising theologian and martyr of Hitler, had in mind when he spoke of a "religion without God."

My experience and feelings can best be described in the terminology of mysticism. A mystic has no need for the construction of a theology or dogma. He can only speak of an experience — of a mystic union with reality, uniquely his own, which really is the essence of all vital and creative religion. To force the religious experience into a theological structure, or to congeal it into a dogma, only robs it of its life-enriching quality. In worship, with the aid of music, singing and the sense of corporate oneness with the worshipping congregation, I can experience my identity with the world about me. Out of it can flow a sense of direction for my conduct on earth; it can help to enlarge the dimension of existence and strengthen the feeling of at-homeness in creation. It can also enlarge a sense of altruism and make one more deeply human.

And what of immortality in this conception of religion? My idea of immortality has always been on shaky grounds in spite of the fact that my parents were totally committed to a physical resurrection, with the firm conviction that on resurrection day the entire Bonikowsky clan would be reunited, except those, of course, who did not make it into heaven because they were "lost." The fact that some seventy-seven billion people have inhabited the earth, since the appearance of homo sapiens, posed no problem for father. Again it was God who would provide the logistics and the space, since for him nothing was impossible. In contrast, I have come to believe with an ancient sage that:

"Death is the termination of life on this planet, and there is no point in dressing it up in a lot of metaphysical jargon."

What has eliminated every last vestige of hesitation for me have been the recent invasions of outer space, the results of astrophysics and the new knowledge we have gained about the universe. It is totally inconceivable to me that this speck of dust, known as planet earth, floating through infinite stellar space, has clinging to it a few billion tiny organisms called humans, who are convinced that some "spiritual" part of them shall defy the known laws of nature and continue on forever! This boggles the imagination and is completely beyond my ken. Buddha is supposed to have laughed while on his death bed, surrounded by his disciples who were trying to console him by assuring him that he had an immortality to look forward to. I will not laugh, but I do have to smile when people elaborate for me their final destinations.

The great Russian philosopher Berdyaev was not sure of his immortality either, but he was quite certain about his purpose on earth. If there should be an immortality, he knew what he would do if it should materialize. He declared that if he should get to heaven, the first thing he would have to do is to look around to see if any of the people with whom he had had a cup of tea a short time ago and the people with whom he had shared the afternoon bus, were there. And if they were absent, he would request to be allowed to go to the other place to find out whether they needed any help. For him there was no heaven where one could not give assistance to the derelicts, the abused and the needy members of the human family.

We have either forgotten or do not realize that our conception of man, the ultimate crown of creation, and our traditional theology had their origin in the primitive Biblical conception of a flat earth; the cosmological three-layer cake, with the sky above, the earth in the middle, and the waters or hell below. The earth was anchored in the center of the universe and all else revolved around it. That is all gone. Copernicus took care of that. The fact is that we are all spinning through outer space, clinging to one of the smallest planets in our Milky Way, with the rest of the universe knowing nothing about us. What we need is a new theology, and a new conception of man that starts with these intimidating facts and reduces him to his appropriate size. This will require a mature theological mind capable of freeing itself from traditional thinking, and knowledgeable enough to make use of the results of contemporary science and research. Dr. Tillich has made a timid effort which, however, is totally inadequate. I discussed the matter with two German theologians recently, one from the University of Heidelberg and the other from the University of Frankfurt. But they failed to throw any light on the subject. One thought that a book of that sort had been written, but I failed to find a copy of it in Germany. We are very much in need of a new theological perspective on where humanity stands in the face of these new facts. And while I was writing these lines, the latest information on the subject was released by one of the greatest physicists of our time, Stephen Hawking of the University of Cambridge, England. He declares that there is evidence that the universe had no beginning and has no boundaries; that it was not created and will not be destroyed. It simply was and is. And then he poses the question: "What place then for a creator?"

Dr. Schweitzer summarizes my position in these words, "Look at the stars and understand how small our earth is in the universe. Look upon the earth and know how minute man is upon it. The earth existed long before man came upon it. In the history of the universe, man is on the earth for but a second. Who knows but that the earth will circle round the sun once more without man upon it? Therefore we must not place man in the center of the universe."

It is no secret anymore. We know now that in the history of the formation and decay of planets there appeared, for a brief moment, on planet earth the proper temperature, the right amount of moisture and the appropriate combination of chemicals to make possible the emergence of life. But since these conditions are constantly undergoing change, the slightest modification will make life impossible. So, one day, the cosmic silence, which was briefly interrupted by the sound of human voices, will return and all that man has done will be no more. There will be no evidence that he ever existed. The only sound that will continue is "the music of the spheres," of which the Greeks sang in their poetry. And what a pity, it seems, that man, with all his creative potential, has never really learned to enjoy his brief moment on earth; that he spends so much of his available time inflicting pain and suffering on his contemporaries. Should not life's brevity make us less arrogant, more cooperative, more humble and more deeply caring?

After what has been said so far, it would seem reasonable to say "What's the use of it all?" Dostoyevsky has Ivan Karamazov say, "If there is no God, all things are lawful." And many others have raised their voices in support of Ivan. But that is nonsense and not true at all, for nothing has really changed. There are laws in the universe as well as in biological organisms, that do not change, nor do they depend on endorsements from beyond. Whether one believes in God or not, these laws of human well-being remain the same for all biological organisms. Lincoln put it as simply as it can be put when he said, "When I do good, I feel good, when I do bad, I feel bad, and that's my religion." This is a law of biology, completely independent of any system of belief. There is another voice that comes to us out of the dim past of a few thousand years ago, affirming the same belief. "Life is given to him who does what is loved, and death is given to him who does what is hated." These laws have their own existence and do not need metaphysical support. The "moral imperative" of which Kant spoke remains. "Whatsoever a man soweth that shall he also reap," that remains. To achieve a rich and fulfilling life can only be done through love and service, no matter what our *Weltanschauung.* Love will always remain more creative than hate, and forgiveness more fulfilling than revenge. These remain axiomatically.

I was deeply impressed by what I found during my conversations with university students in Russia, most of whom are atheists. Their concern for society, their desire to be of serivce, their sensitivity to injustice, and their readiness to serve their nation were impressive, matching the idealism of those who consider themselves religious. These moral values did not have their origin in a particular notion of God; they had their origin in the culture and in the native quality of the individual. While Christianity, over the centuries, may have increased the reservoir of compassion and kindness among some people, other religions have had similar results, and they are equally to be found among people without any religious pretensions. They do not require extra-terrestrial sources.

E. S. Jones has written a helpful book in this area entitled, *Is the Kingdom of God Realism?*, which once significantly influenced my thinking about the ethical teachings of Jesus. He shows that the Sermon on the Mount does not point at some idealistic goal toward which one should strive. On the contrary, it is a description of how the human organism functions. If we love, life blossoms; if we are generous, life responds and cherishes us. And this law of nature remains the same in all religions, all philosophies or political systems, for atheists and believers alike. In this universe, our home, we are never at liberty to live as we please in the hope of escaping the consequences. The ethical teachings of Jesus remain as relevant as ever, since they have their biological structure in human nature itself and are as dependable as the laws of physics.

It has been a long and painful journey, both for humanity and for myself. Mankind has just survived the bloodiest century in human history. Never before has brutality reached such dimensions, and involved so many millions. And all of this after man has been around for a million years. My rational faculties are no longer able to either cope with or explain these dimensions of evil. From South Africa to Palestine, from India to Ireland, from Afghanistan to Central America, and even the cities of America, the killing never ends. How can anyone justify this or have any part in it? Yet the vast majority seem to feel quite at home in such an environment and freely participate in it. Some hold that our economy can only prosper with a large war industry. For thousands of years every society has had its War Department. There is no evidence there has ever been a Department of Peace. This gives ample evidence of man's obsession with brutality and self-destruction. It pervades the atmosphere and every child born into such a culture, learns to live and participate in inhuman behavior, and may become incapable of seeing the human enterprise in any other terms.

Yet in every age there have been some gentle voices, appealing to the conscience of the individual, and begging for pity, mercy and kindness. There are many volumes that have been written in behalf of a nobler humanity. Here and there are small groups whose sensitivity and idealism enables them to rise above their time and culture, to see and dream of a day when war shall be no more. They are to be found in every age, beginning with some of the prophets of Israel. They are the ones that have kept the dream alive. And their number seems to be on the increase. Fortunately, there are new forces propelling mankind into a planetary society, often against his will. These forces have no regard for traditional national borders or any other fences man has built. Among them is economic interdependence. No nation can make it on its own today, largely because of the impact of scientific research, man-made satellites, acid rain, contagious diseases like AIDS, the Chernobyls, and much, much more. These no longer ask if man is ready to join the cosmic family. His only option is to join or be eliminated. What idealism, religion or the saints have failed to accomplish, is now in the hands of cosmic forces. There is no turning back. We are forced to become our brother's keeper,. I quote the great British historian, Arnold Toynbee, who confirms my hope: "Whatever our present day governments may do or say, the tide now making for the unification of the world will go rolling on irresistibly. I do not believe it can be stopped before it has brought mankind one or the other of two alternatives: union or self-destruction."

Against this background the drama of my life has been enacted. Out of these events and other available materials, I have had to carve my destiny and to become the person I now am. It is against this background that I had to decide what role I was going to play in the drama of human existence, and what contribution I could make toward the enrichment of life, in return for my debt to so many. I am especially grateful to those who have enriched my life through stimulating conversation; to the philosophers of all ages who have given me hours of pleasure and who have encouraged my search; for the many books that have become my dear companions; and to the schools that did not lose hope. After years of effort, the time came when I knew that I had arrived. There was no longer anxiety, no more elemental questions needing solution. I no longer had to beg for attention. People responded in a stimulating and loving way. All the parts of creation had fallen into place, so that I could feel at home in it and cherish it. I had found my intellectual and metaphysical home. I have come a long way from the little boy, lost in the forest in Poland, telling the people who found me that I was hungry and wanted to go home. The home the boy was looking for was a place of familiar objects, of shelter, of playmates and of safety. The home I ultimately found fulfilled those childhood longings, but grown to cosmic proportions. I now am at home in the universe.

Let me close with two quotations which reflect my point of view. The first comes from a philosopher and the other from a poet. Said Voltaire, who has given me many hours of pleasure, *"I die loving my friends, not hating my enemies, and detesting superstition."*

And Alfred Lord Tennyson wrote:

> *Flower in the crannied wall,*
> *I pluck you out of the crannies,*
> *I hold you here, root and all, in my hand.*
> *Little flower -- but if I could understand*
> *What you are, root and all, and all in all,*
> *I would know what God and man is.*

Index

ABOUT THE AUTHOR

Exiled to Siberia in 1915 at the age of five with his entire village, Oscar Bonny and his family endured great suffering and privation. One morning they awoke to find their home and entire village buried in a snowstorm. His minister father kept his congregation together in Siberia throughout the civil war, revolution, and under Stalin's harsh rule. In 1920 they fled to escape famine in a freight train falsely labeled cargo. Horrendous stories circulated. A note found in a vacant village read:

"There is little to tell. We ate our bread. When that was gone we mixed our last flour with grass and weeds. When that was gone we ate dogs, cats, rats and birds. When they were gone, we ate each other. Then we died."

They remained in the Ukraine until 1926, finally escaping to Latvia, then Canada. In Saskatchewan the unschooled, extraordinary young man fell in love with an 18-year old girl who rejected him because she could never "marry an illiterate". Driven to thoughts of suicide one dark night in the woods, he determined instead to get an education and wrote to a small N.Y. college.

Initially rejected, the following summer he appeared at the school doorsteps to beg for a chance. The Dean, a kindly soul, agreed. Years of intense work and suffering followed, after which he graduated with honors, to the Dean's astonishment. He received a Bachelor of Divinity in 1937, a BA from Sioux Falls College in 1939, and a Masters Degree from Oberlin College in 1943. He also pursued advanced studies at the University of Heidelberg, Germany.

Ordained a Baptist minister, he later joined the theologically liberal Congregational Church (now United Church of Christ), serving as minister for:

Pilgrim Congregational Church, Cleveland, 1943-1948; First Congregational Church, Anthony KS, 1948-1952; Rosedale Congregational Church, Kansas City, 1952-1962; Topeka Congregational Church, 1962-1968; and as Executive Secretary for Baltimore Monthly Meeting of Friends, Homewood, 1968-1975.

His ministry was marked by a strong concern for social justice, and early civil rights activism. Later, he became a much sought after public speaker, lecturing about his life in Siberia, the USSR, and serving as a speaker for the UN.

He lives with his wife, Jane, in a home he remodeled himself, close to Johns Hopkins University, is a member of the Eclectic Club and Philosophical Society, and remains a vigorous doubles tennis player.